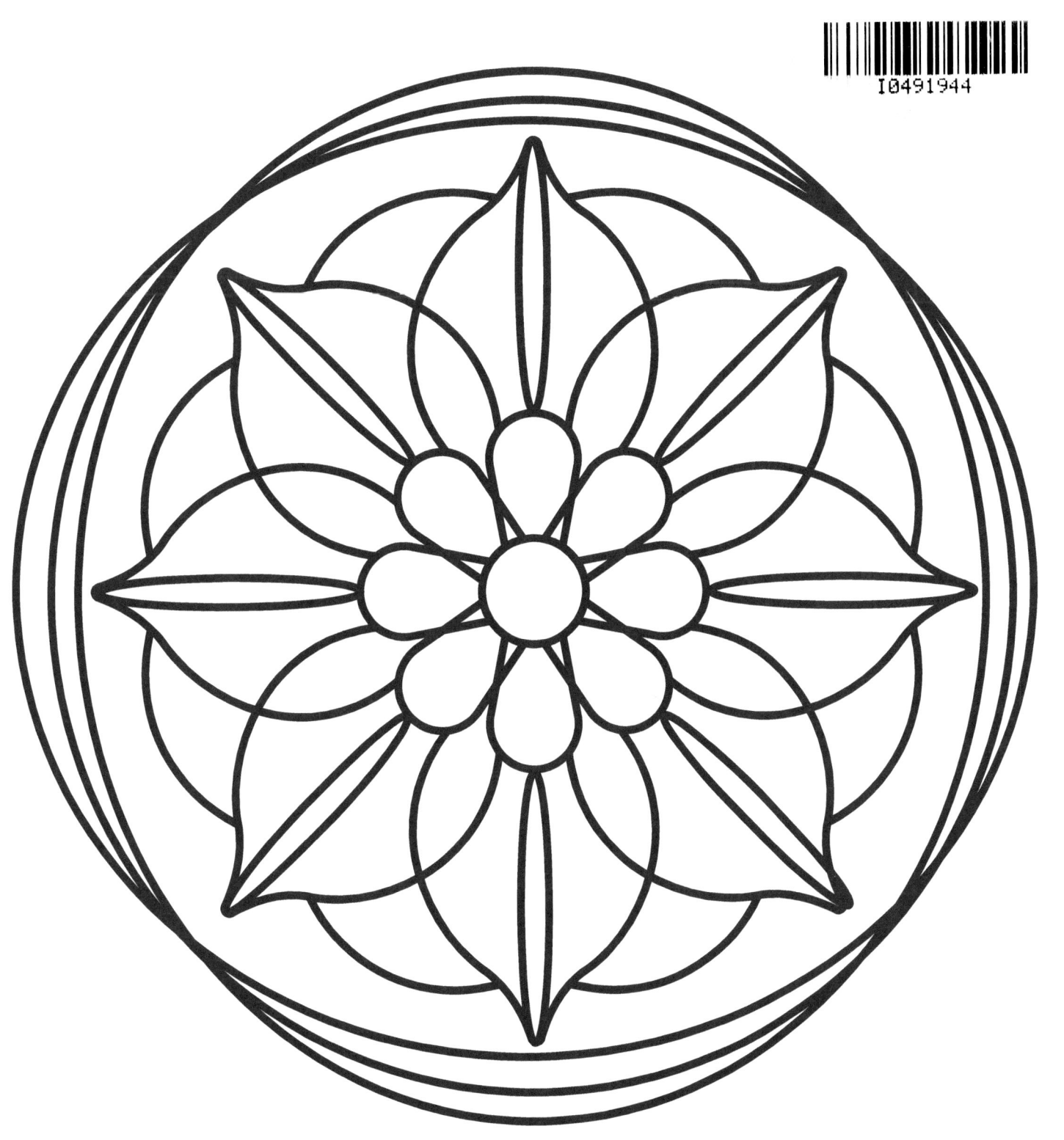

HELLO

by Lili Marlenn

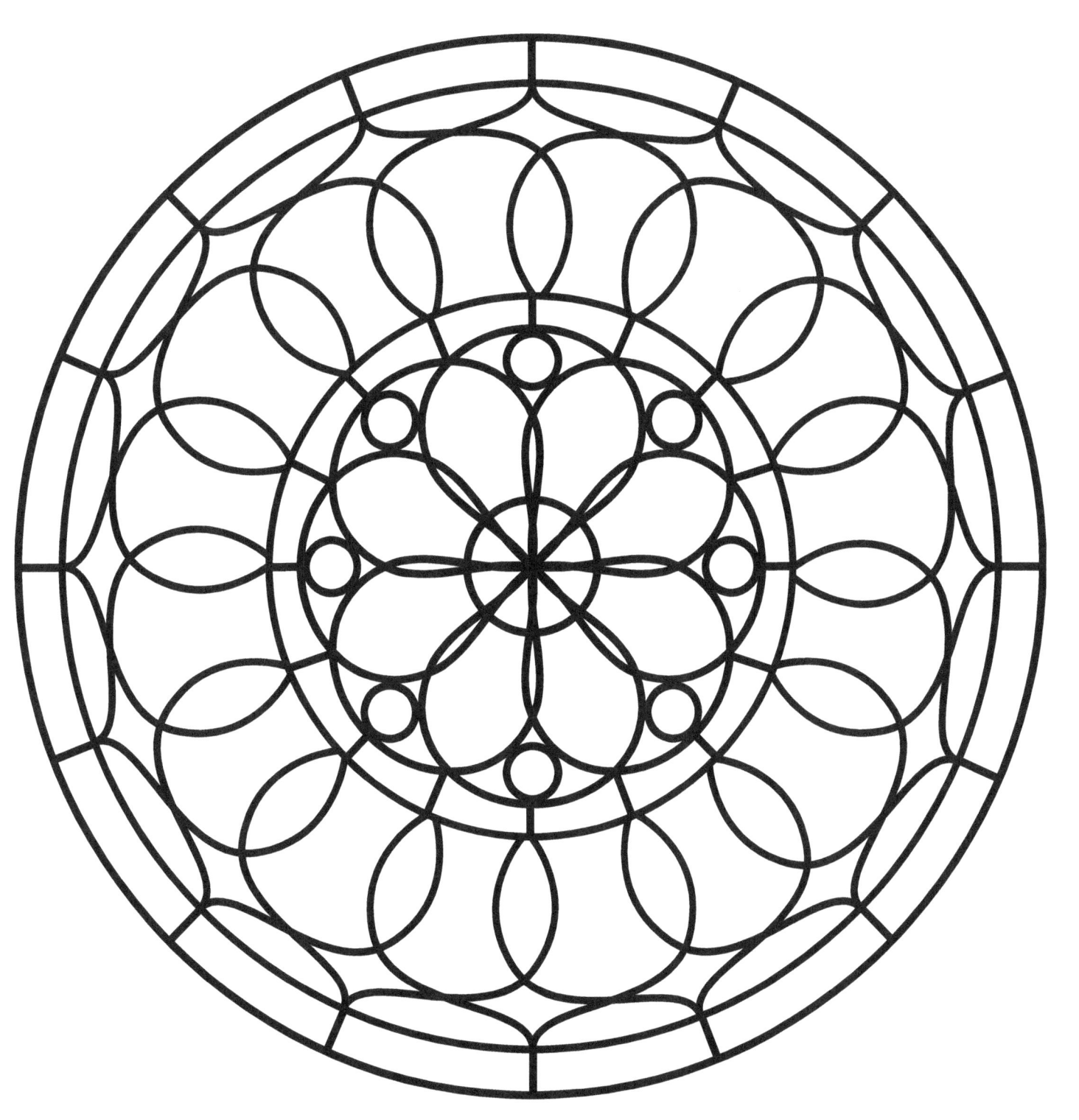

WHAT'S YOUR NAME?

by Lili Marlenn

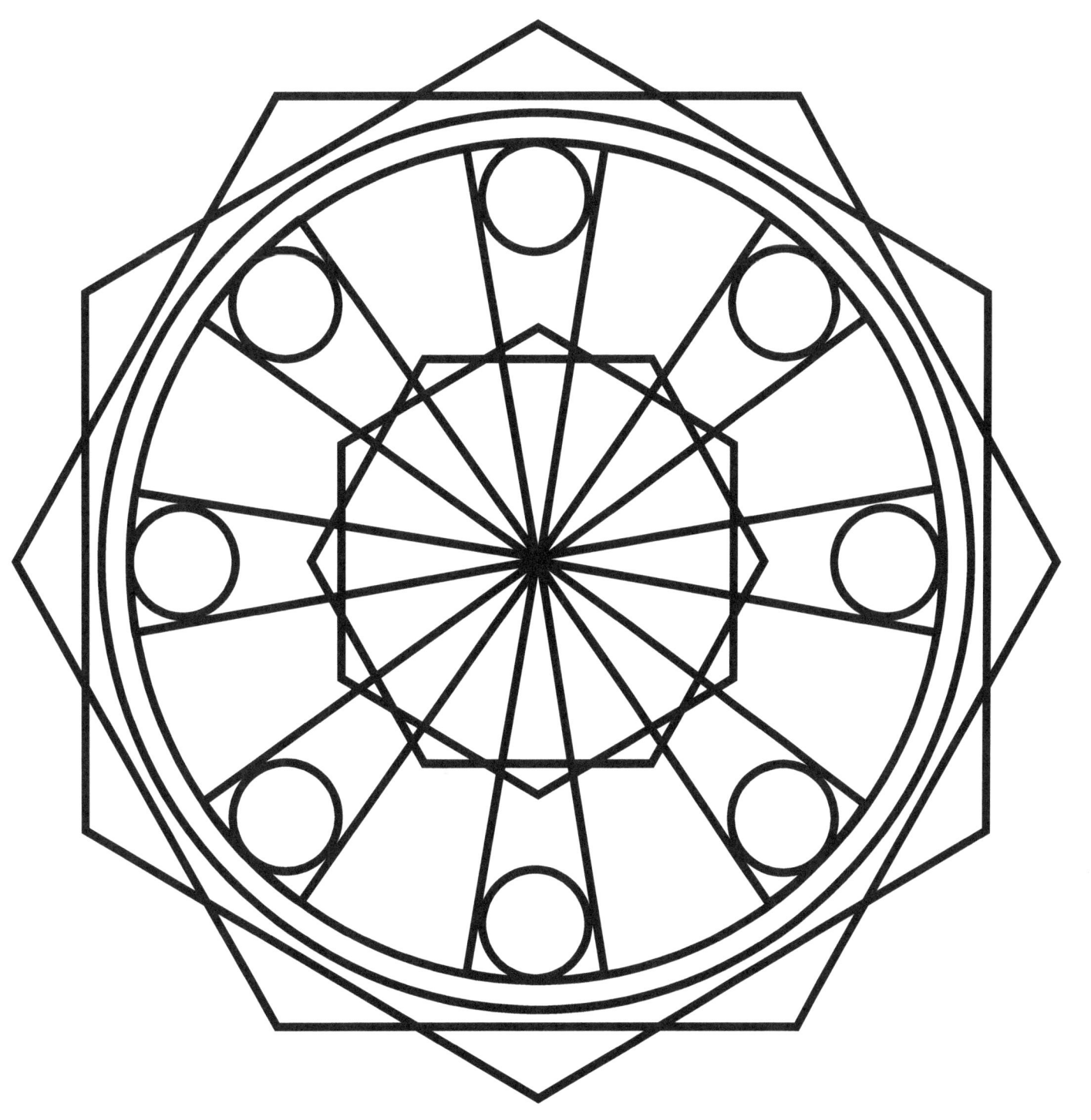

HOW ARE YOU?

by Lili
Marlenn

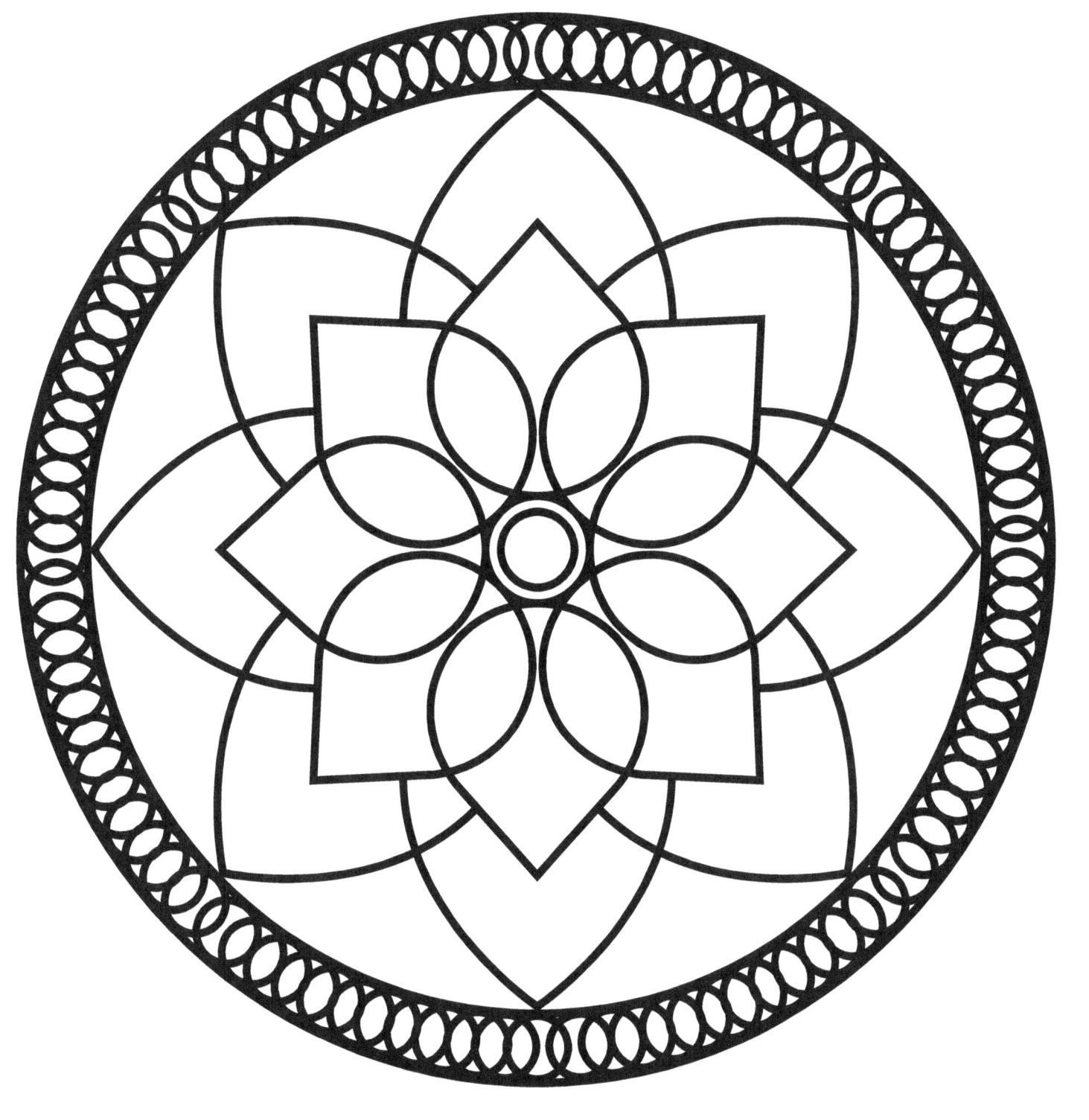

GOOD LUCK

by Lili Marlenn

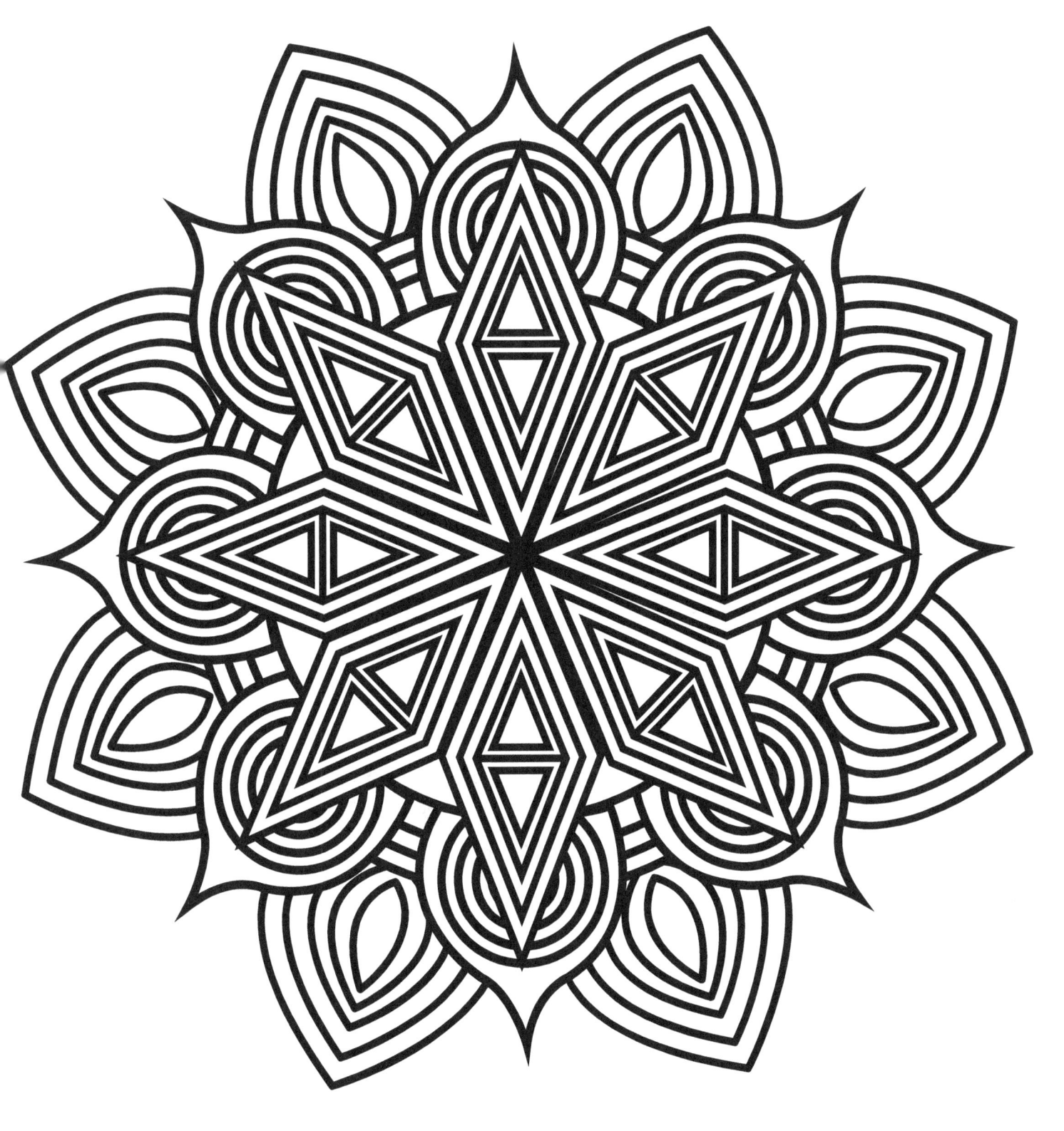

EVERYDAY
IS A CHANCE

by Lili
Marlenn

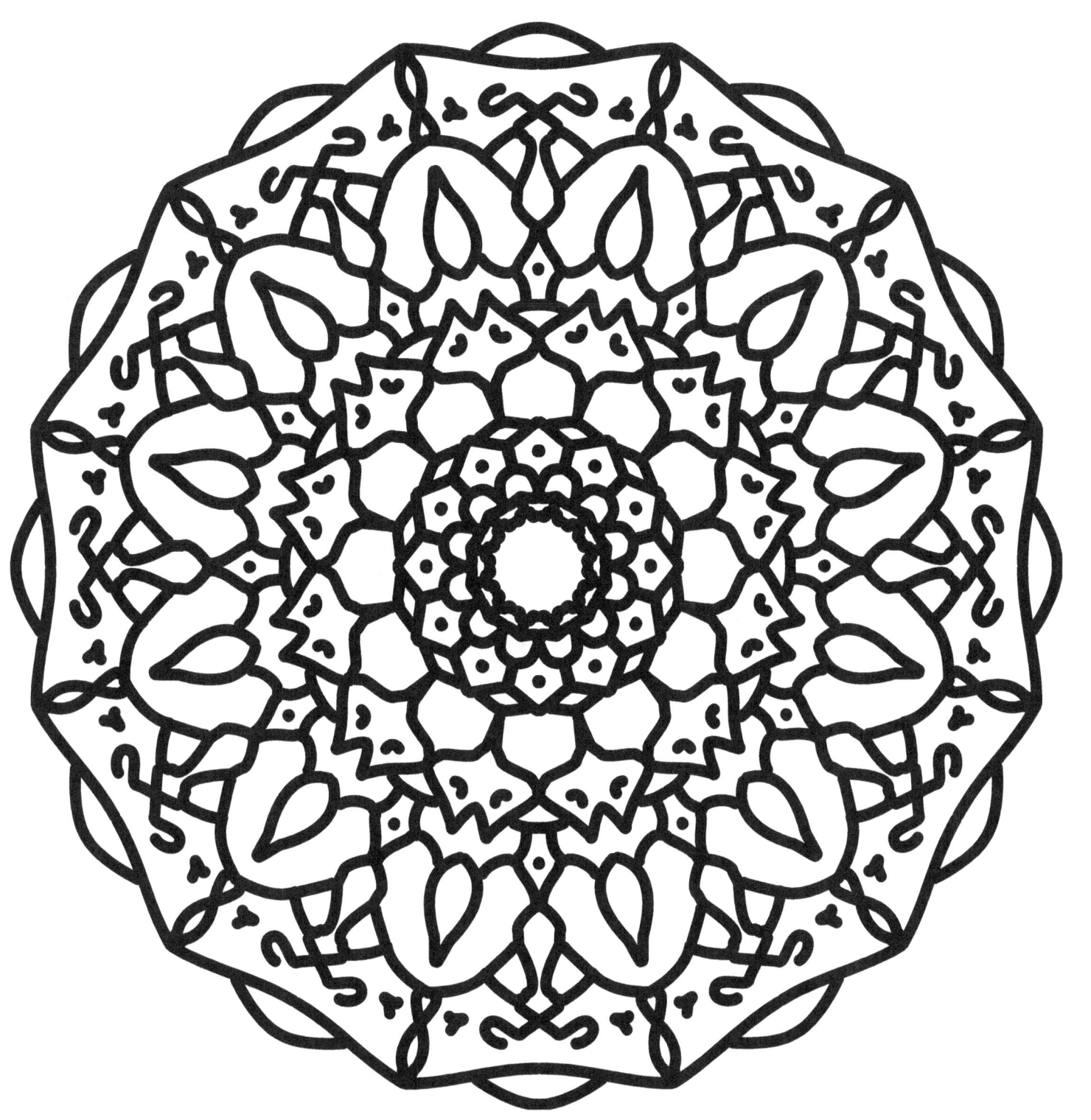

LOVE AND LOVE

by Lili
Marlenn

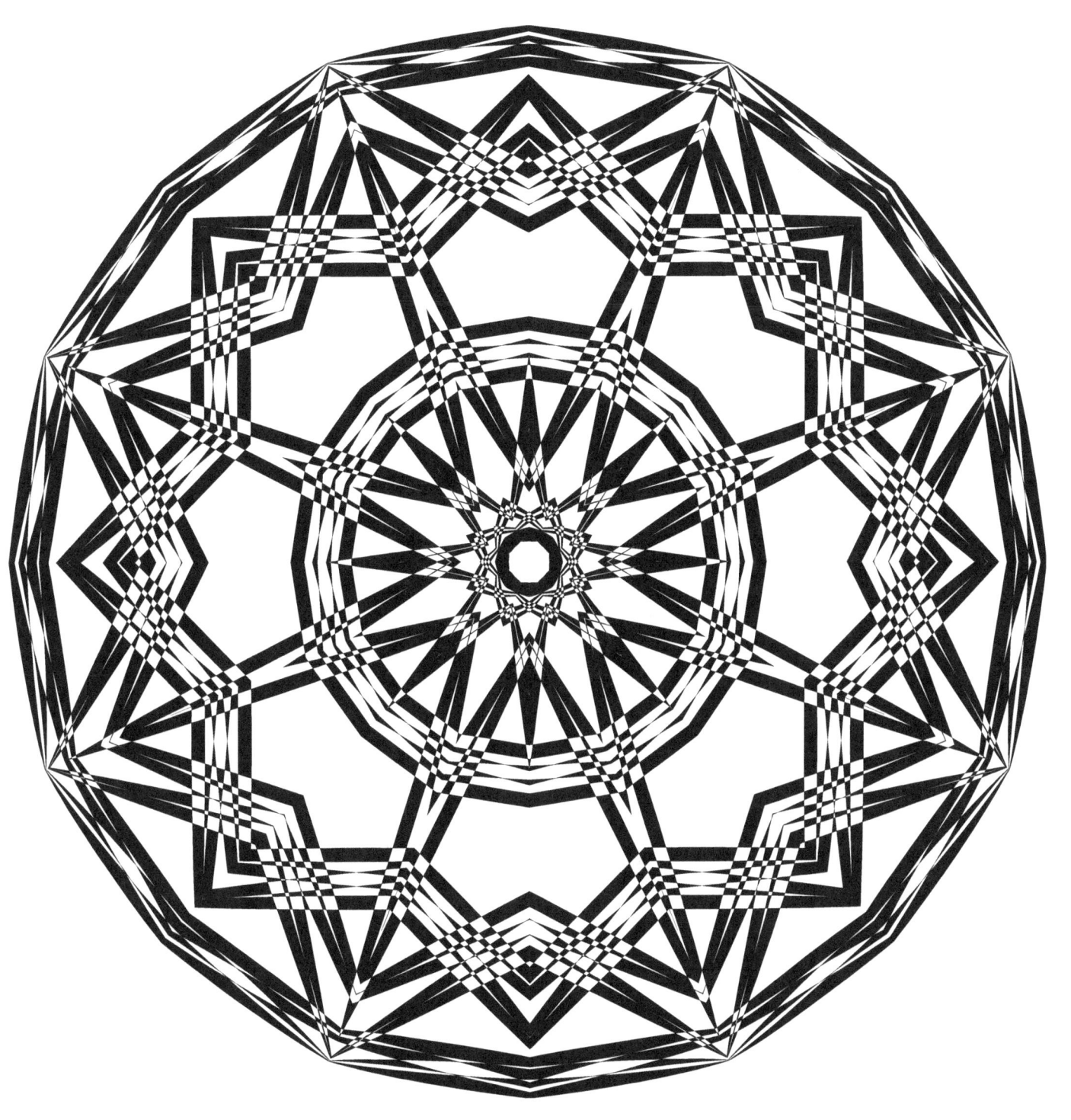

SMILE!

by Lili Marlenn

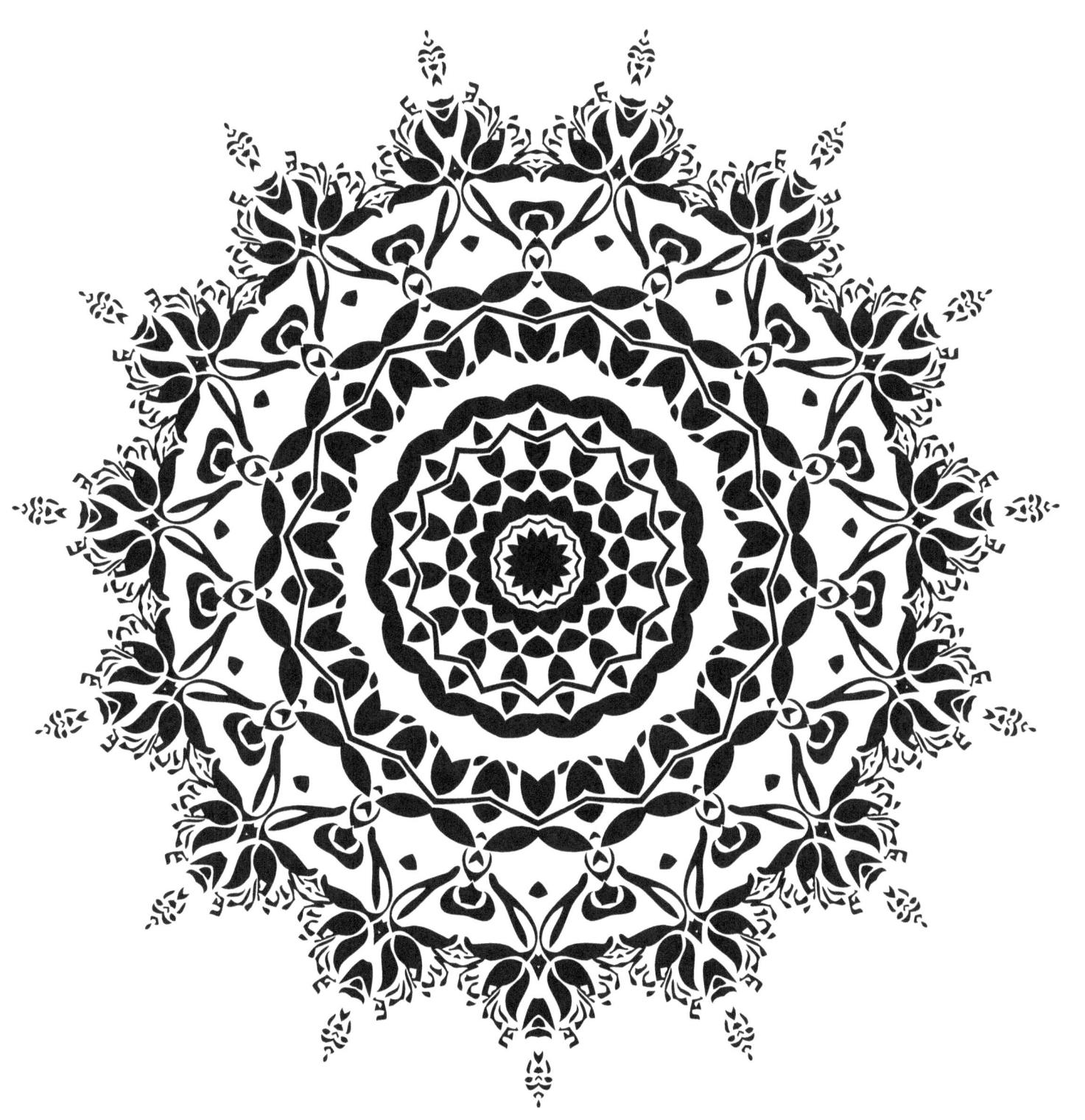

FEEL GOOD

by Lili
Marlenn

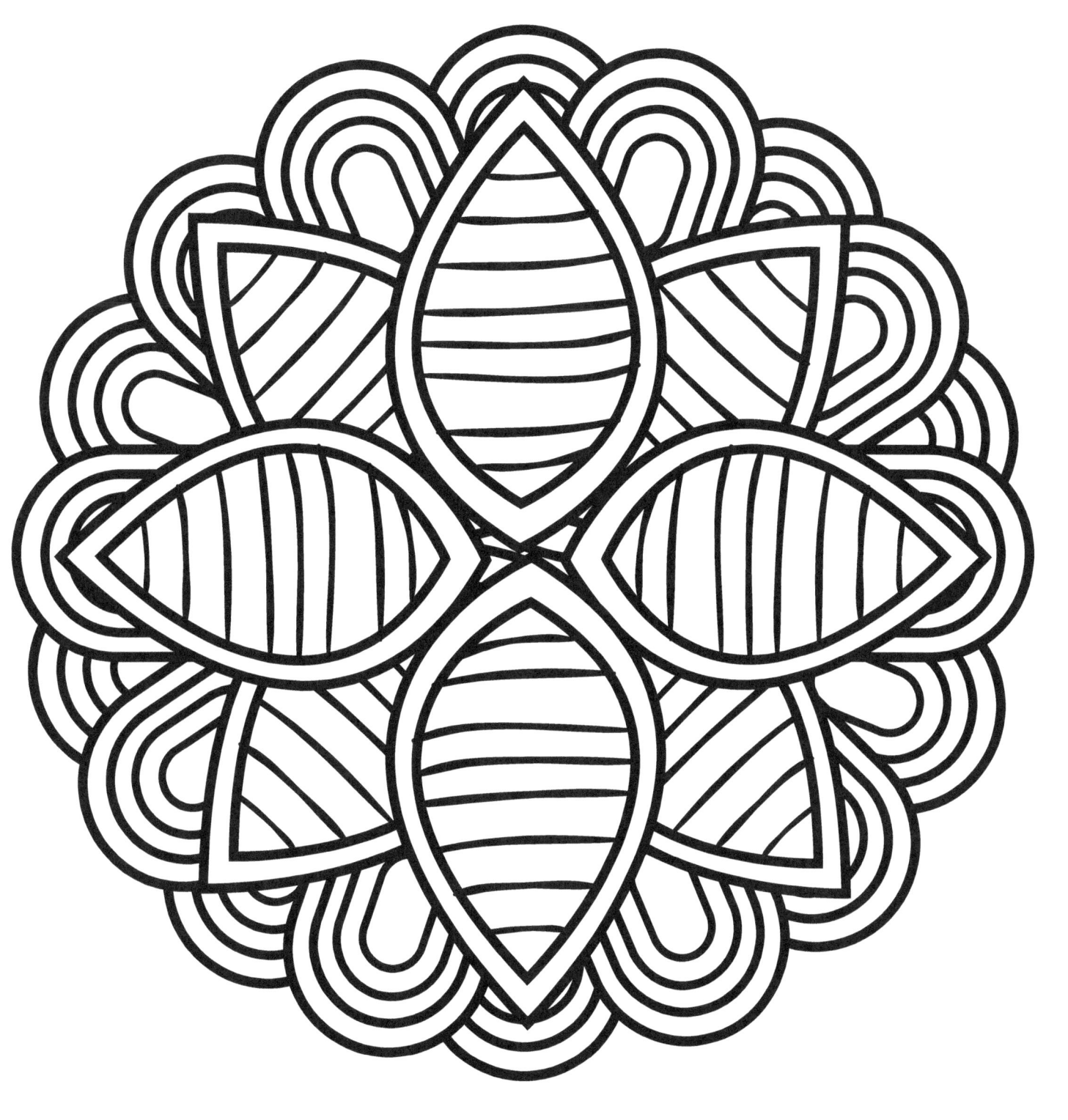

BEAUTY

by Lili
Marlenn

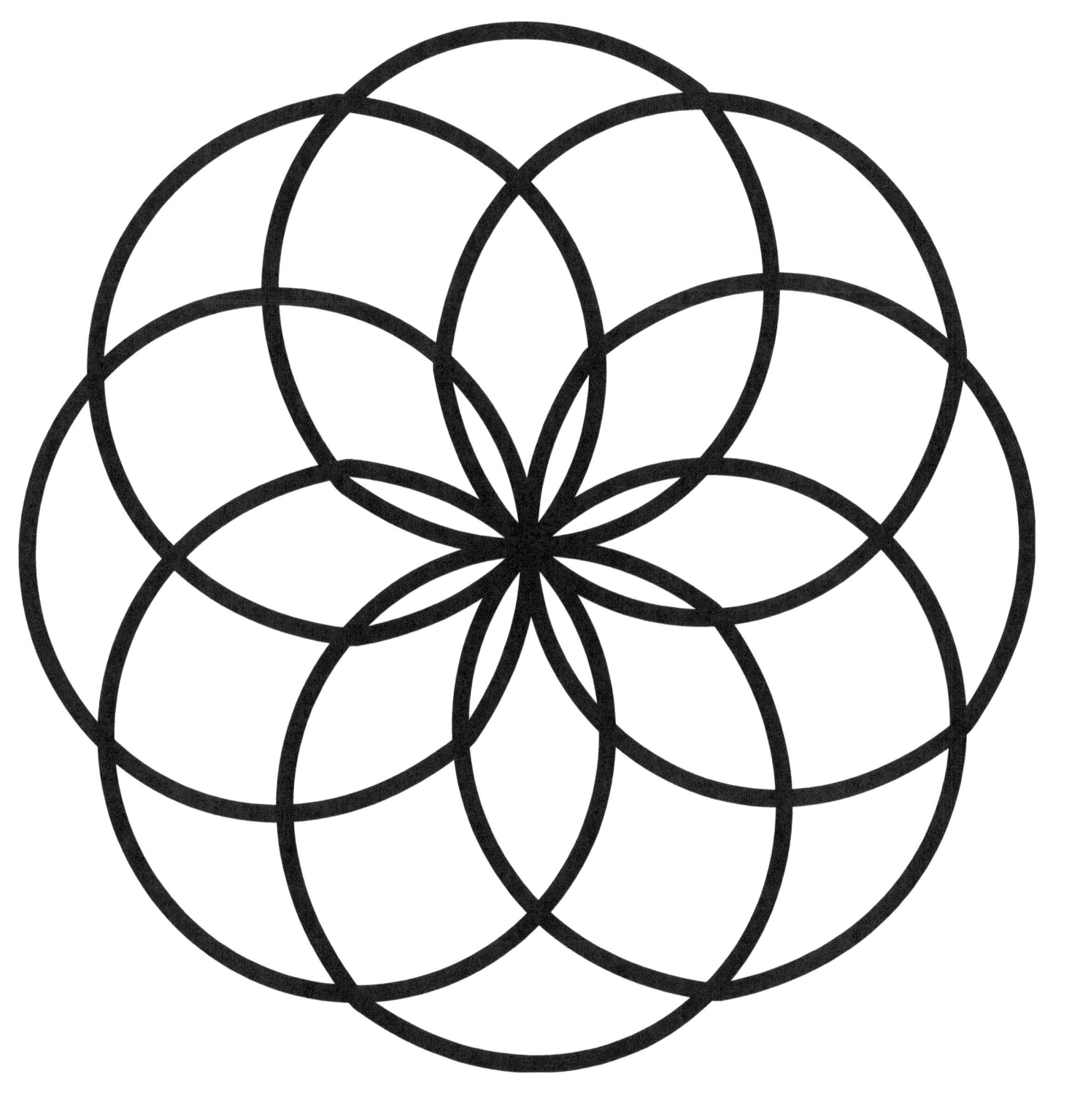

YOU CAN

by Lili
Marlenn

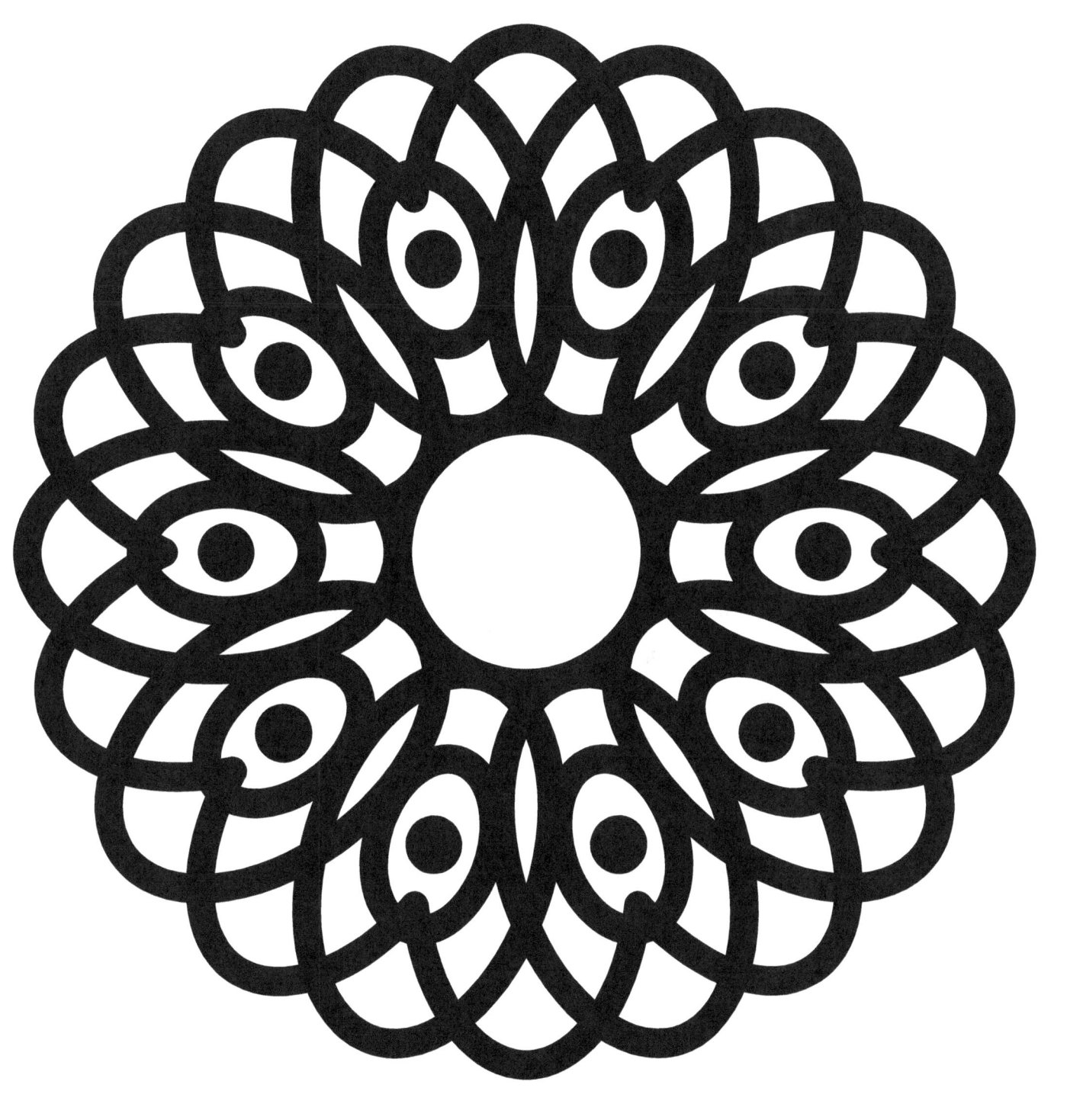

YOU WILL

by Lili
Marlenn

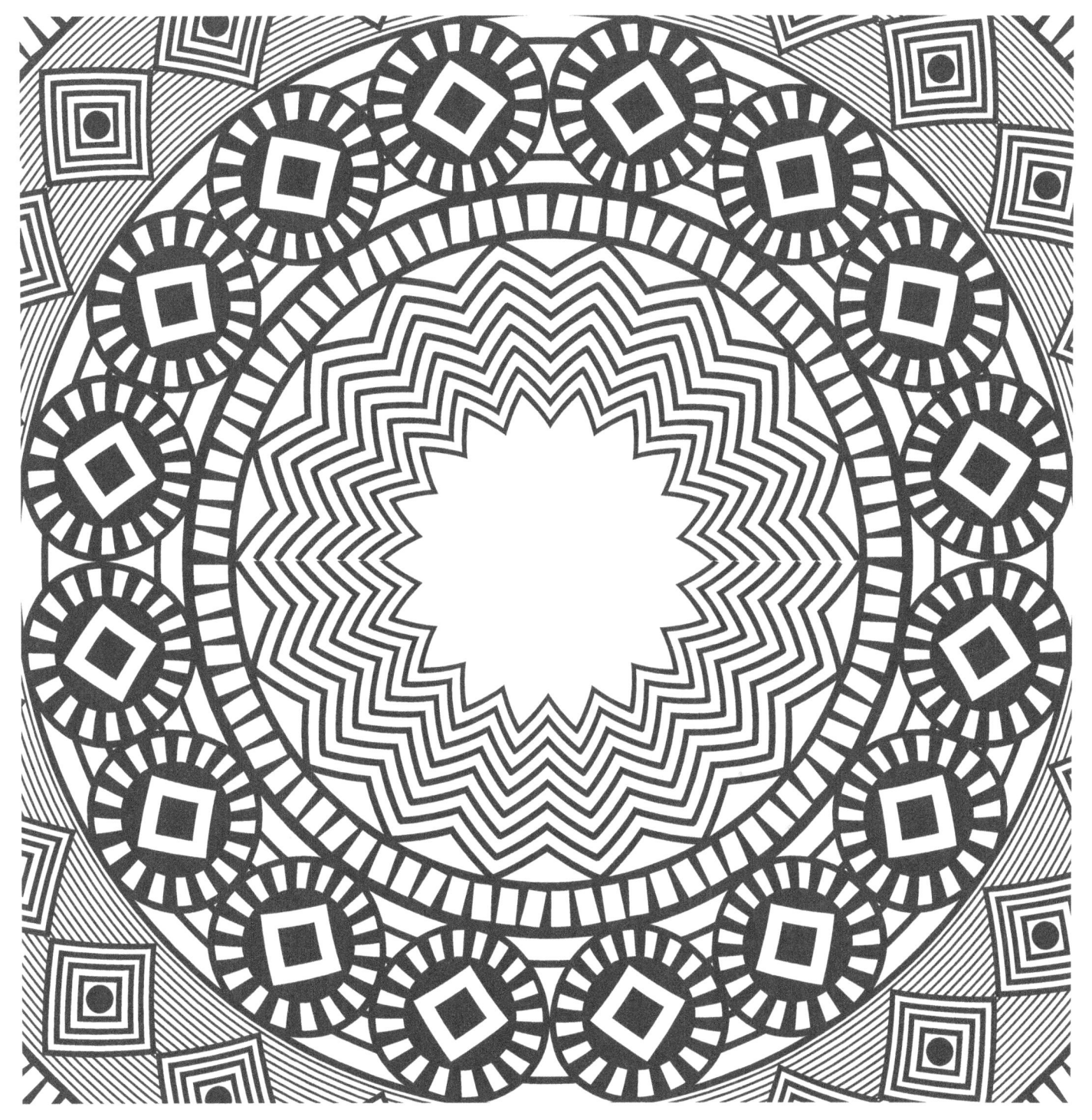

THANK YOU

by Lili
Marlenn

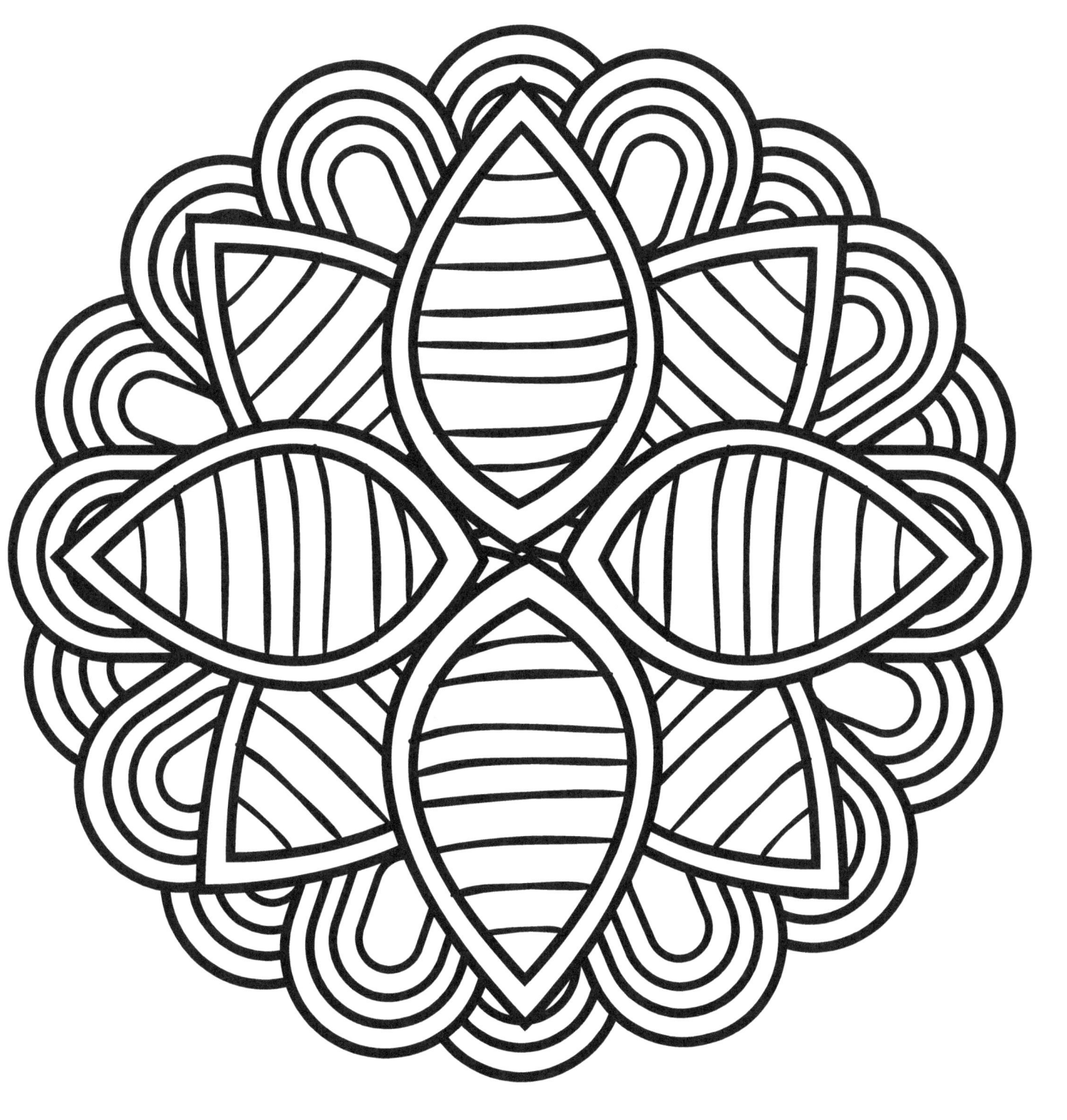

KEEP CALM

by Lili
Marlenn

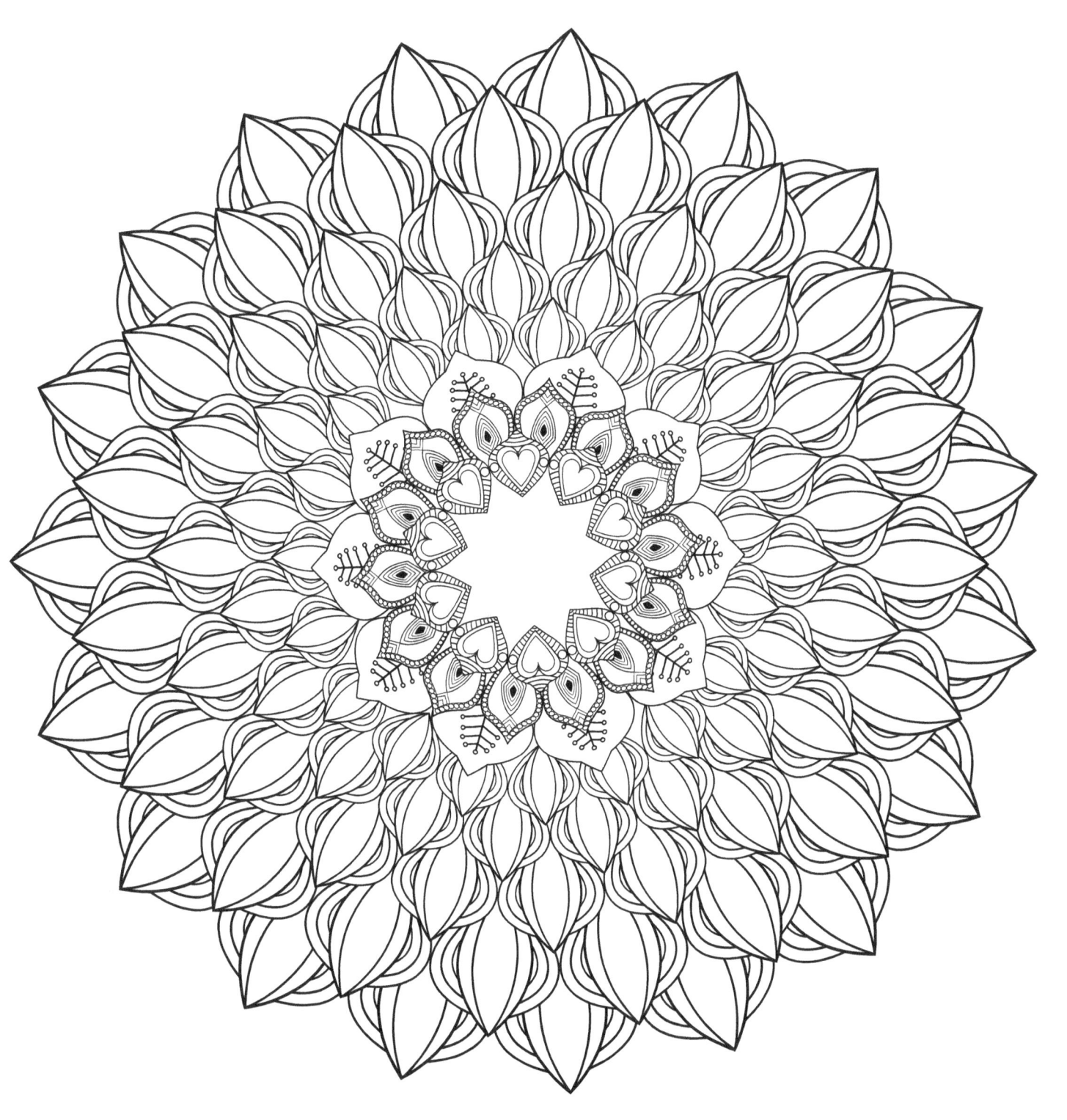

EAT SMTH
GOOD

by Lili Marlenn

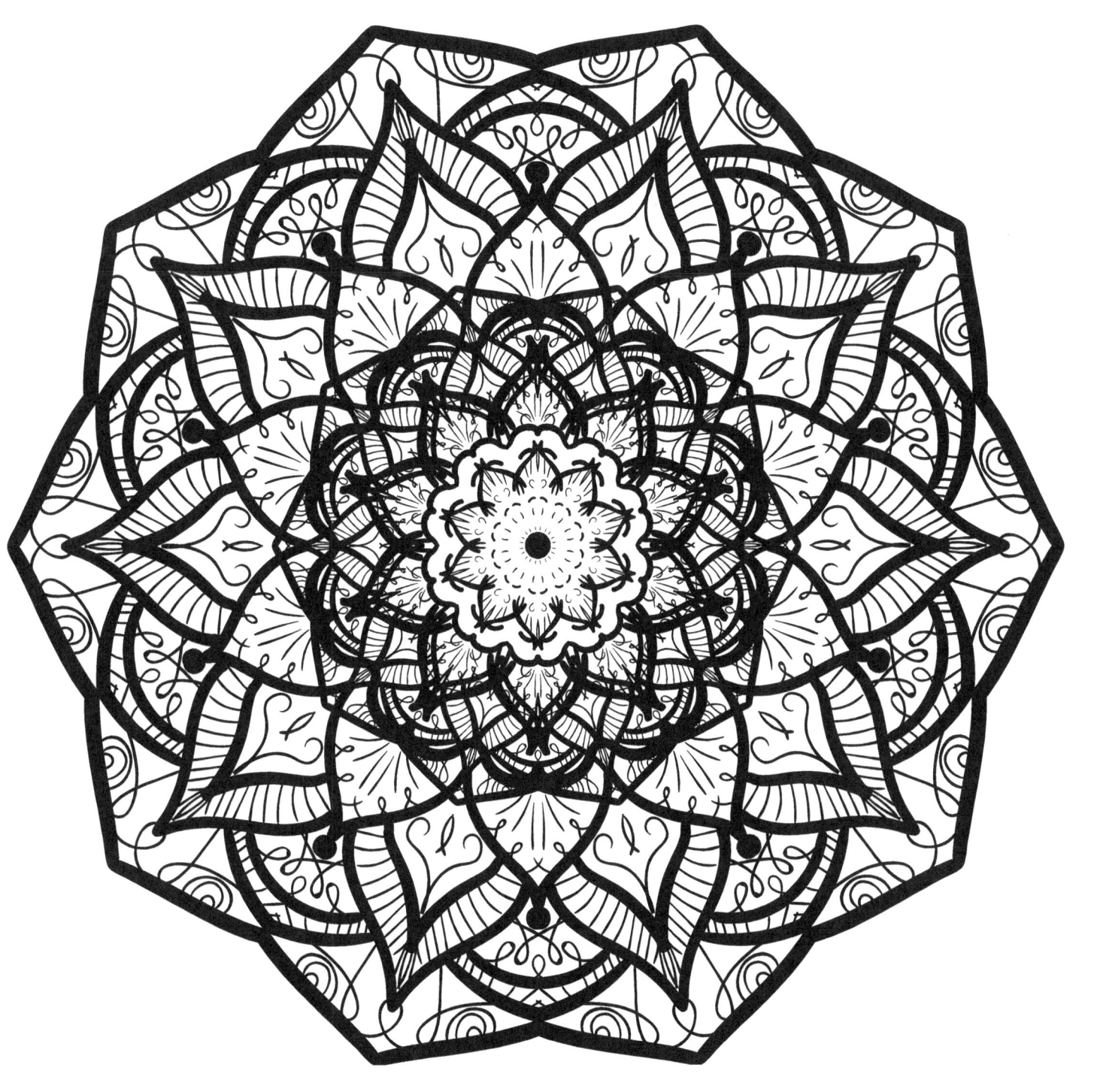

HAVE A NICE DAY

by Lili
Marlenn

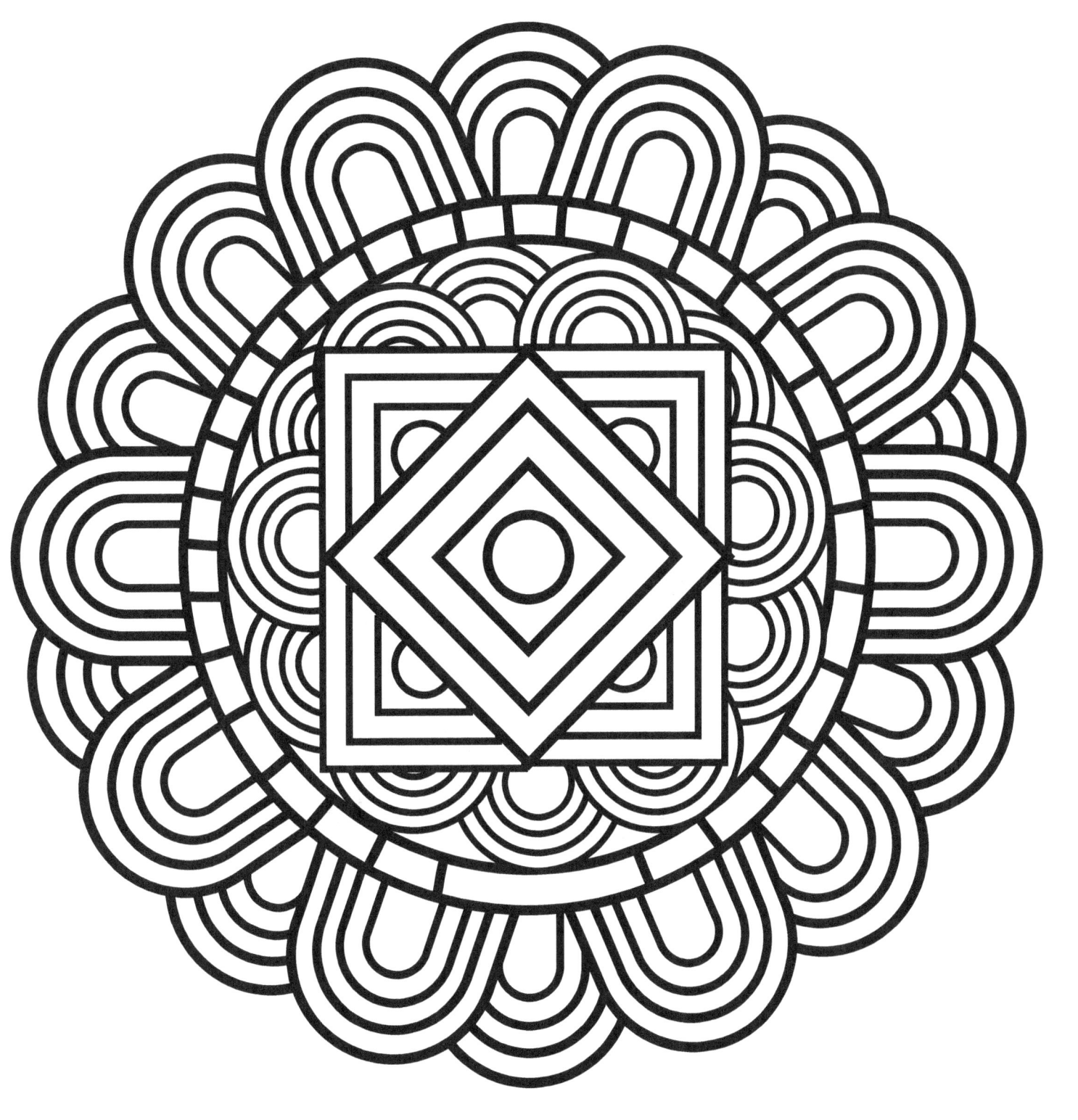

GOOD VIBES

by Lili
Marlenn

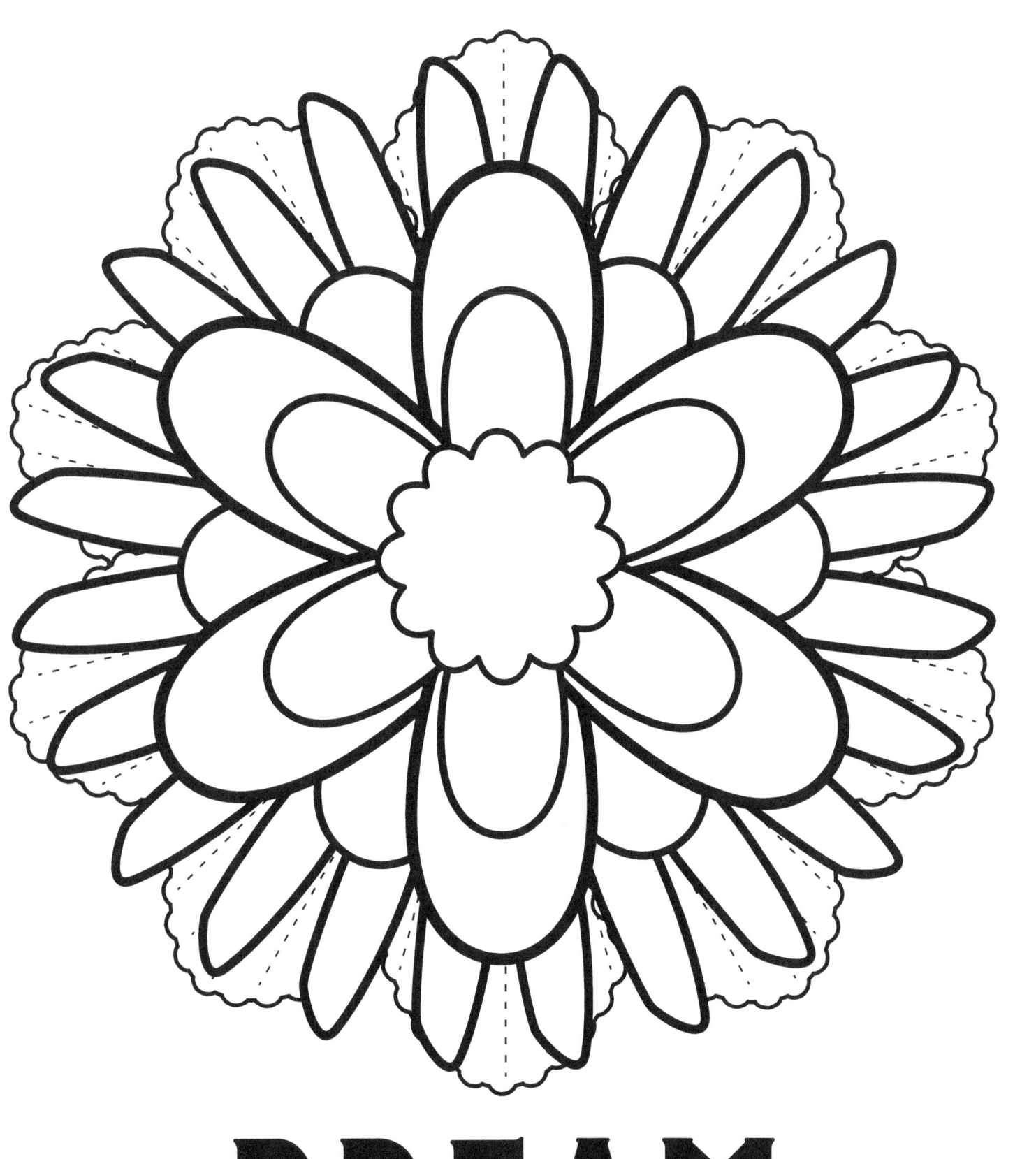

DREAM
DREAM

by Lili
Marlenn

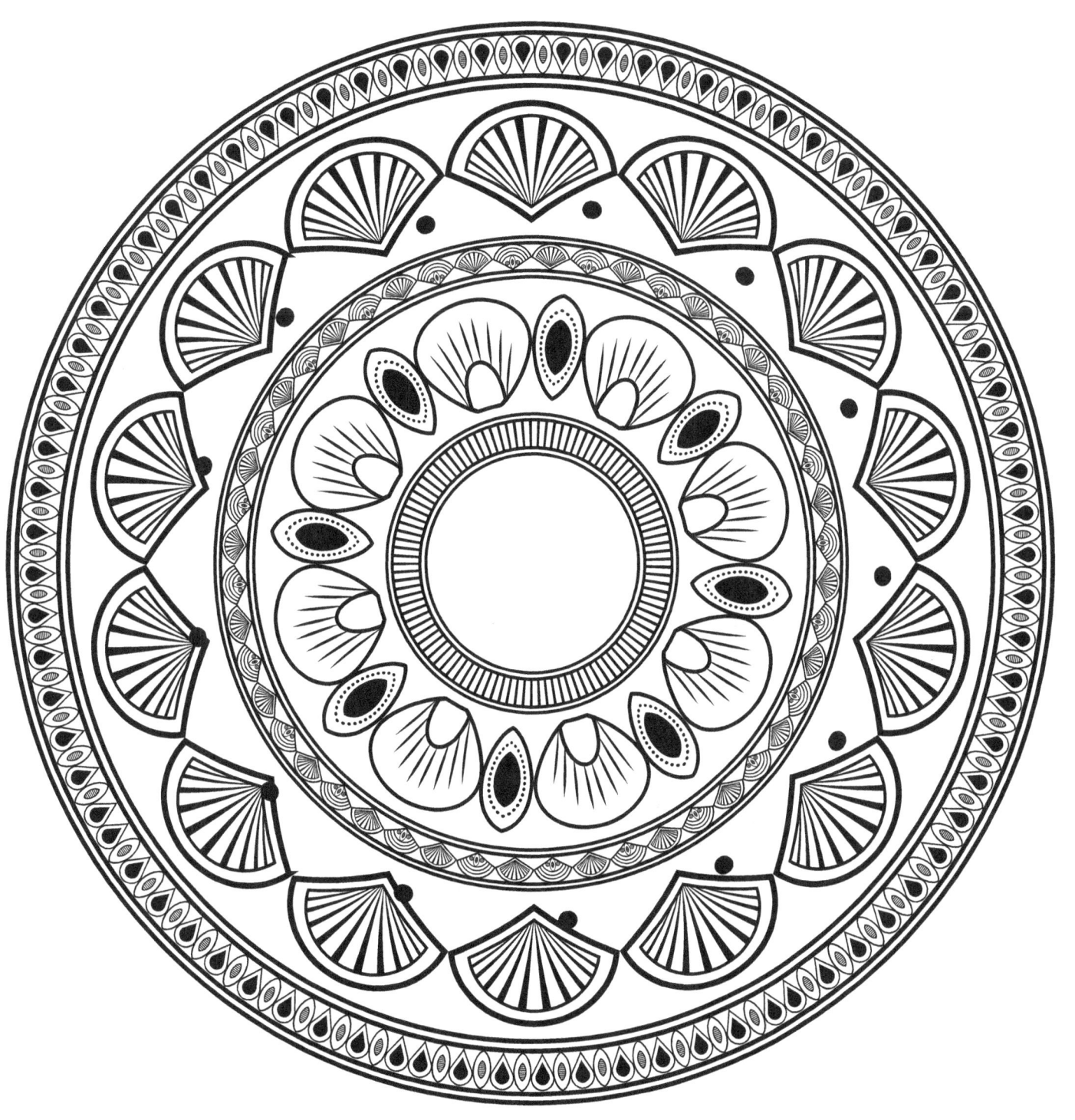

BE FREE

by Lili Marlenn

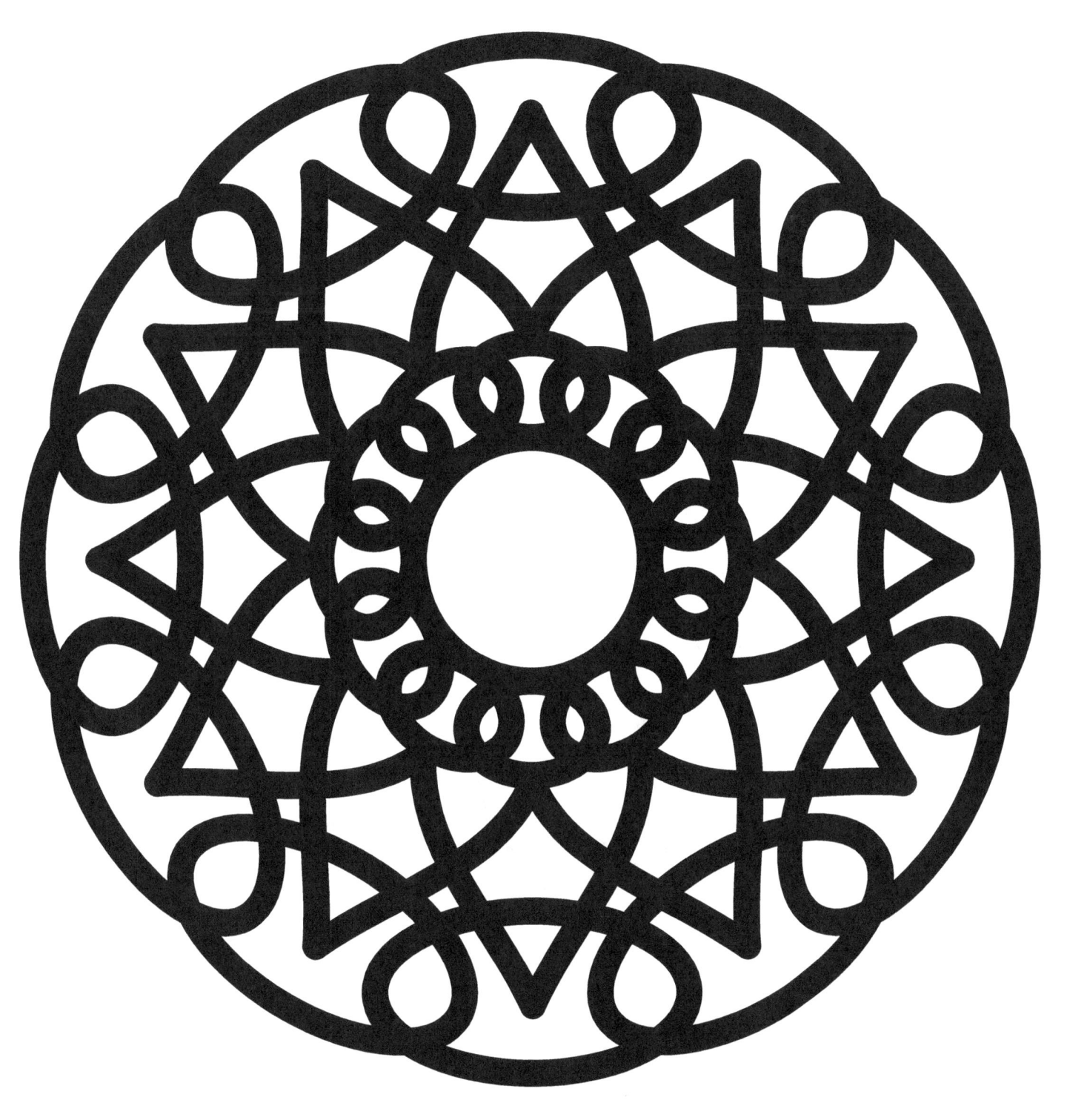

ONE LIFE ONE CHANCE

by Lili
Marlenn

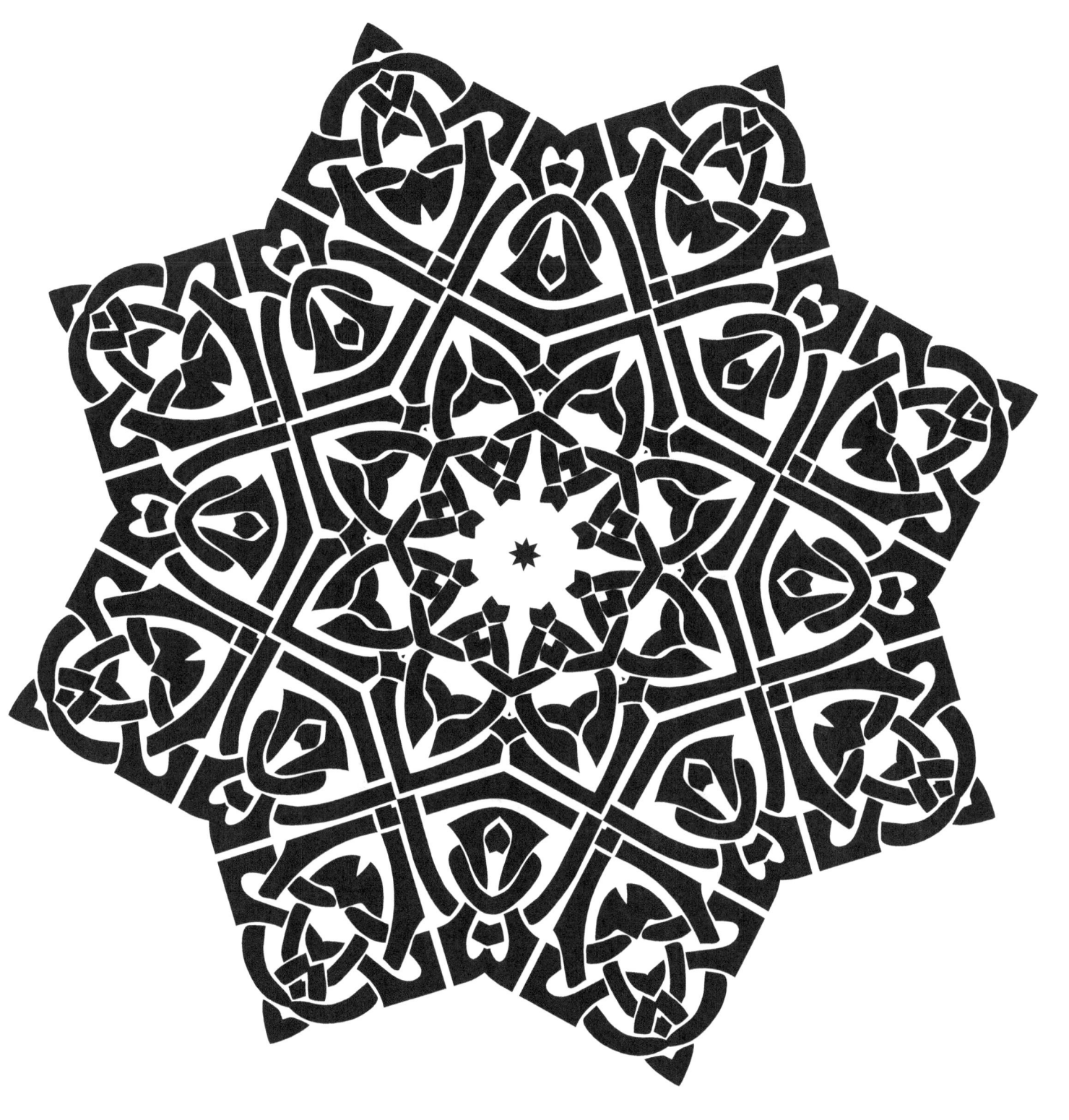

TAKE IT

by Lili
Marlenn

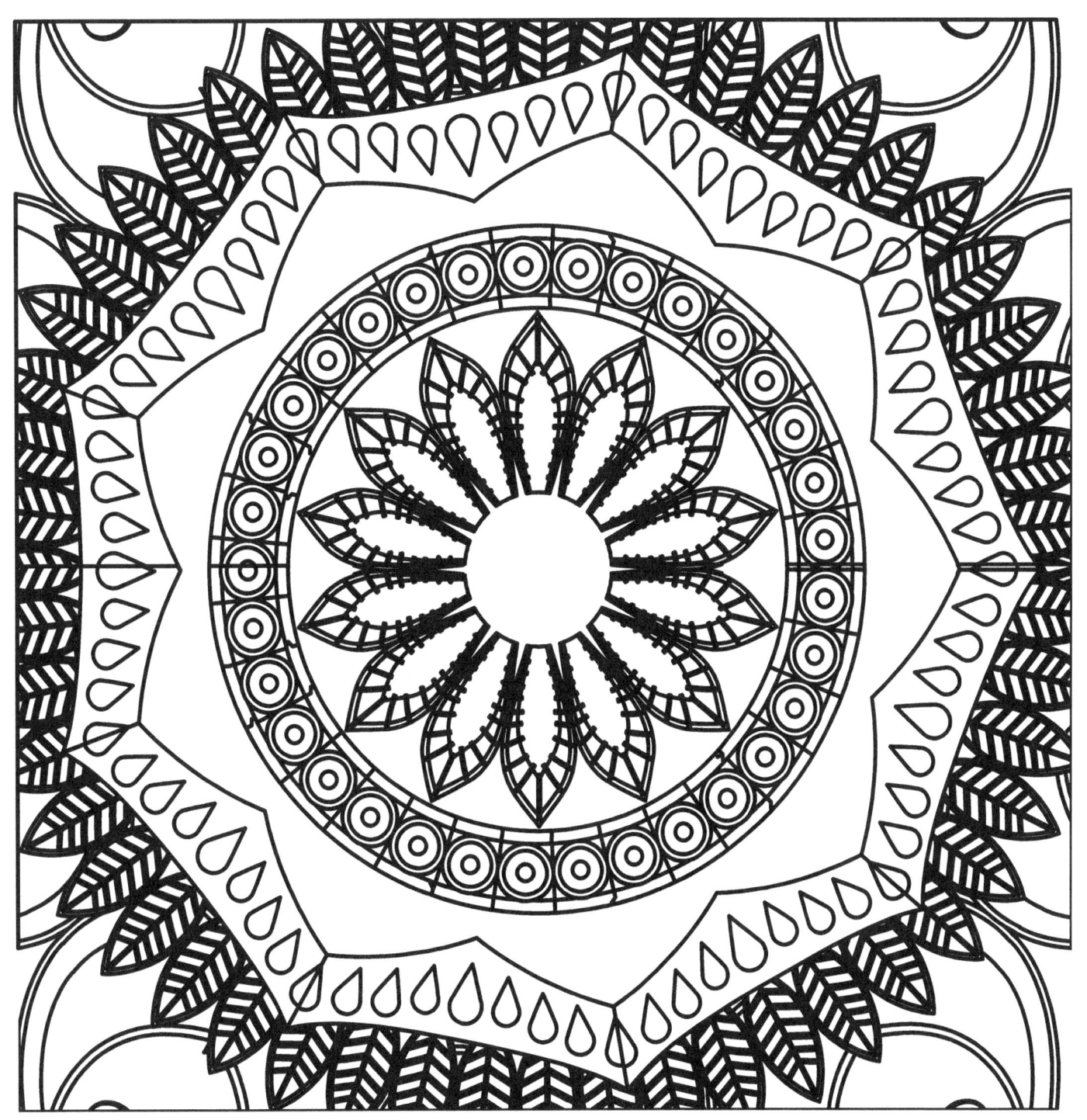

FLY AWAY

by Lili
Marlenn

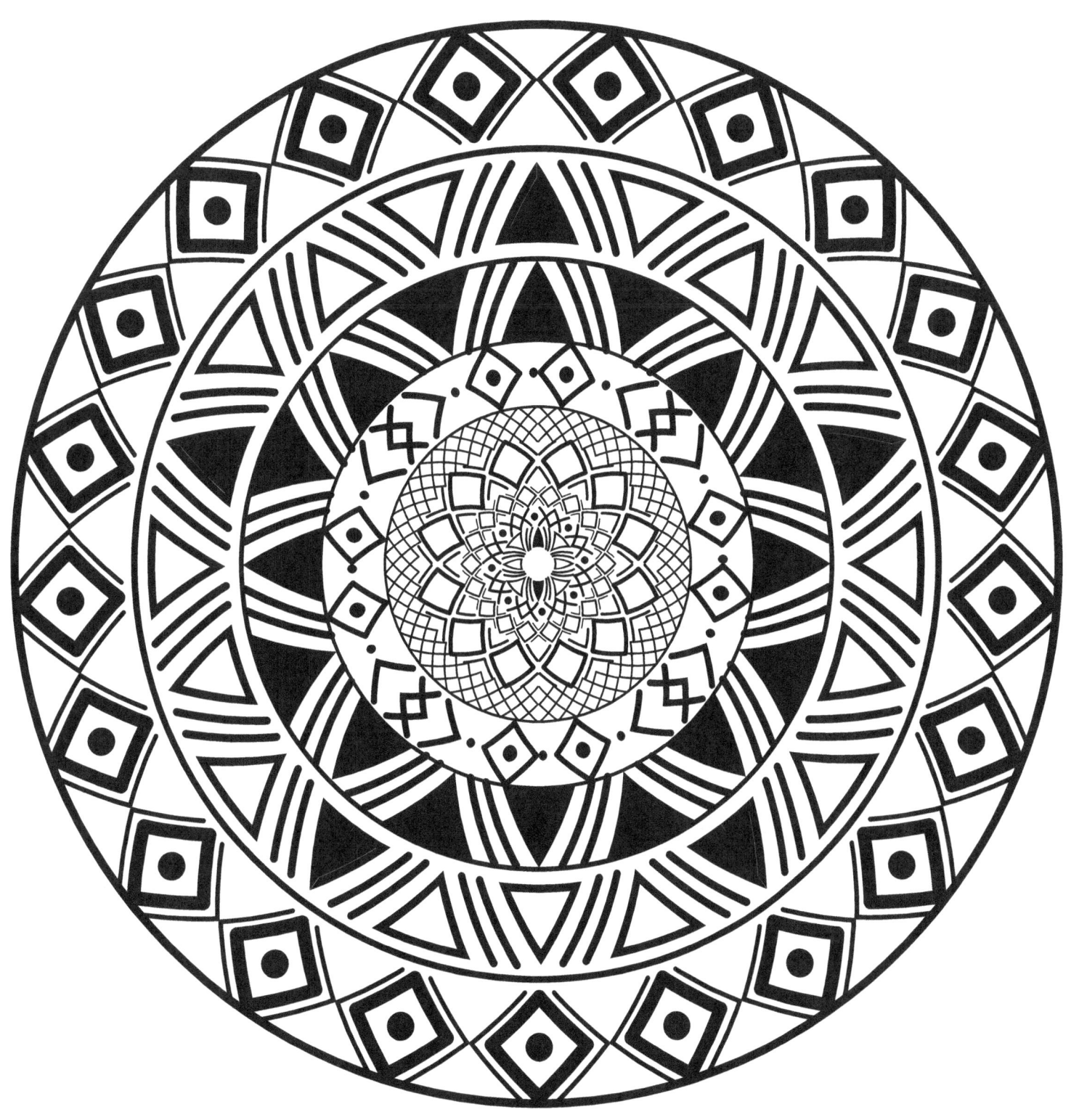

DON'T WORRY
BE HAPPY

by Lili
Marlenn

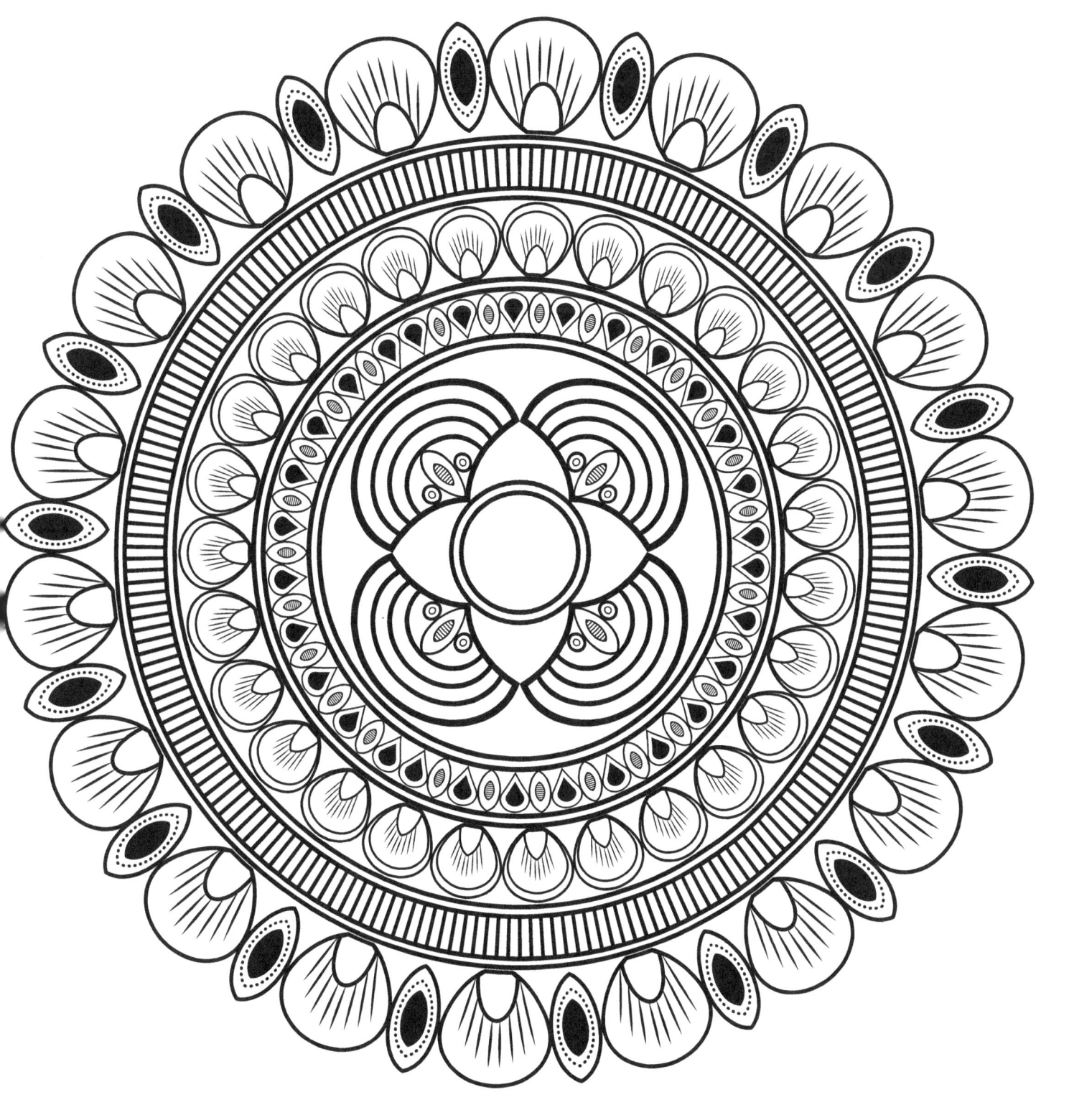

FAVOURITE DAY

by Lili
Marlenn

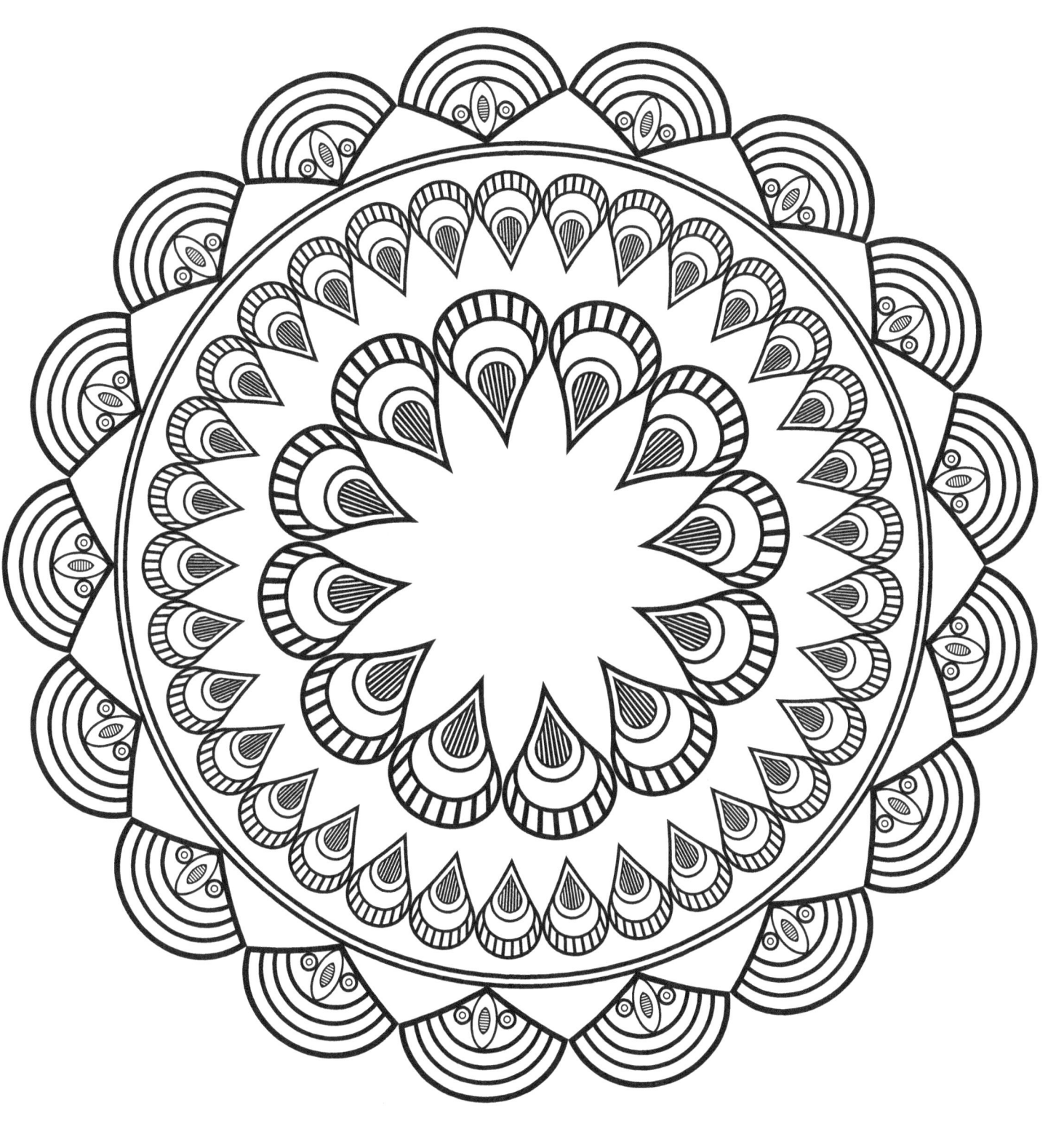

TASTY

by Lili
Marlenn

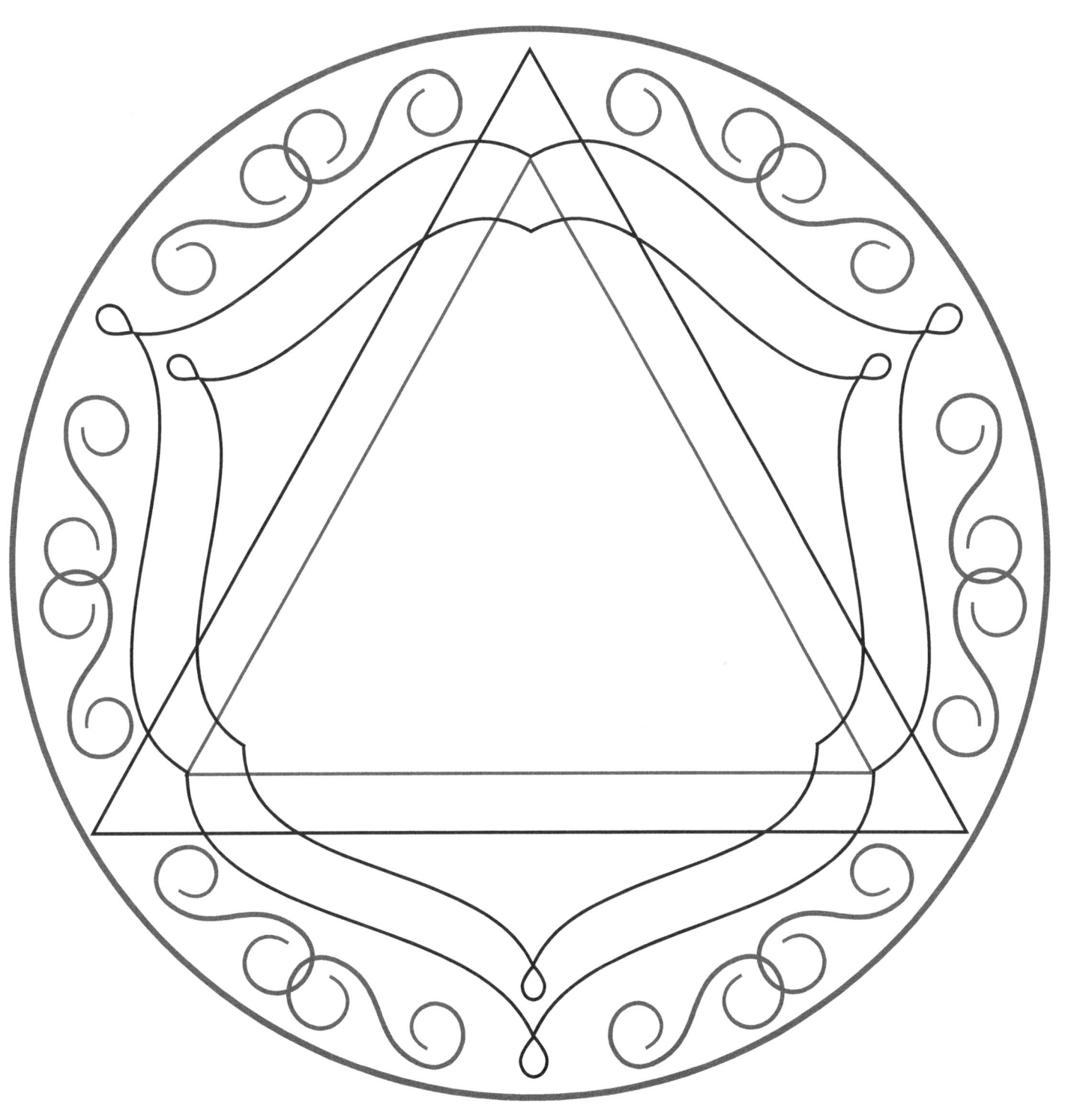

BLESS YOU

by Lili Marlenn

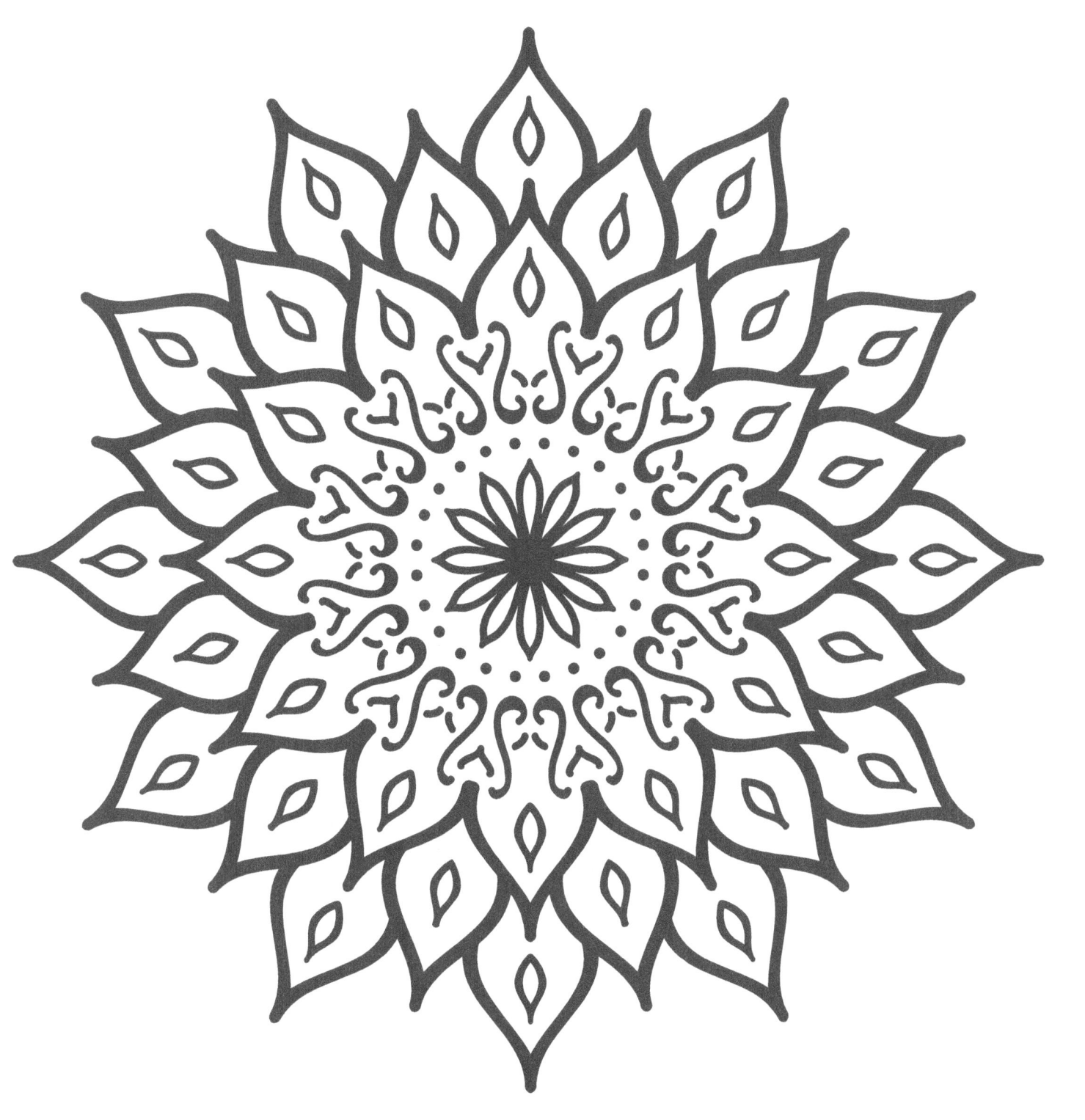

SHALL WE DANCE

by Lili
Marlenn

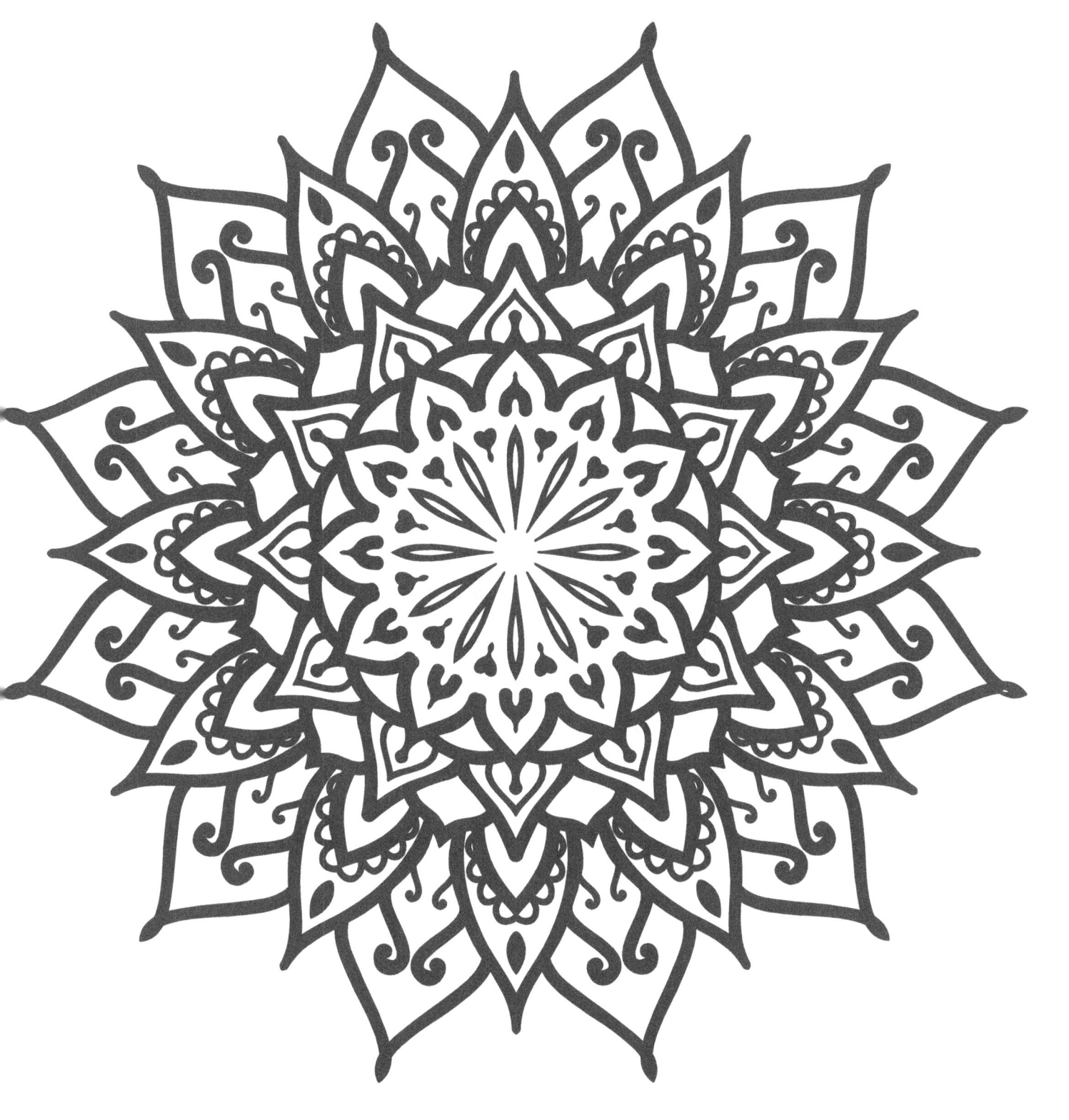

TOTALLY

by Lili
Marlenn

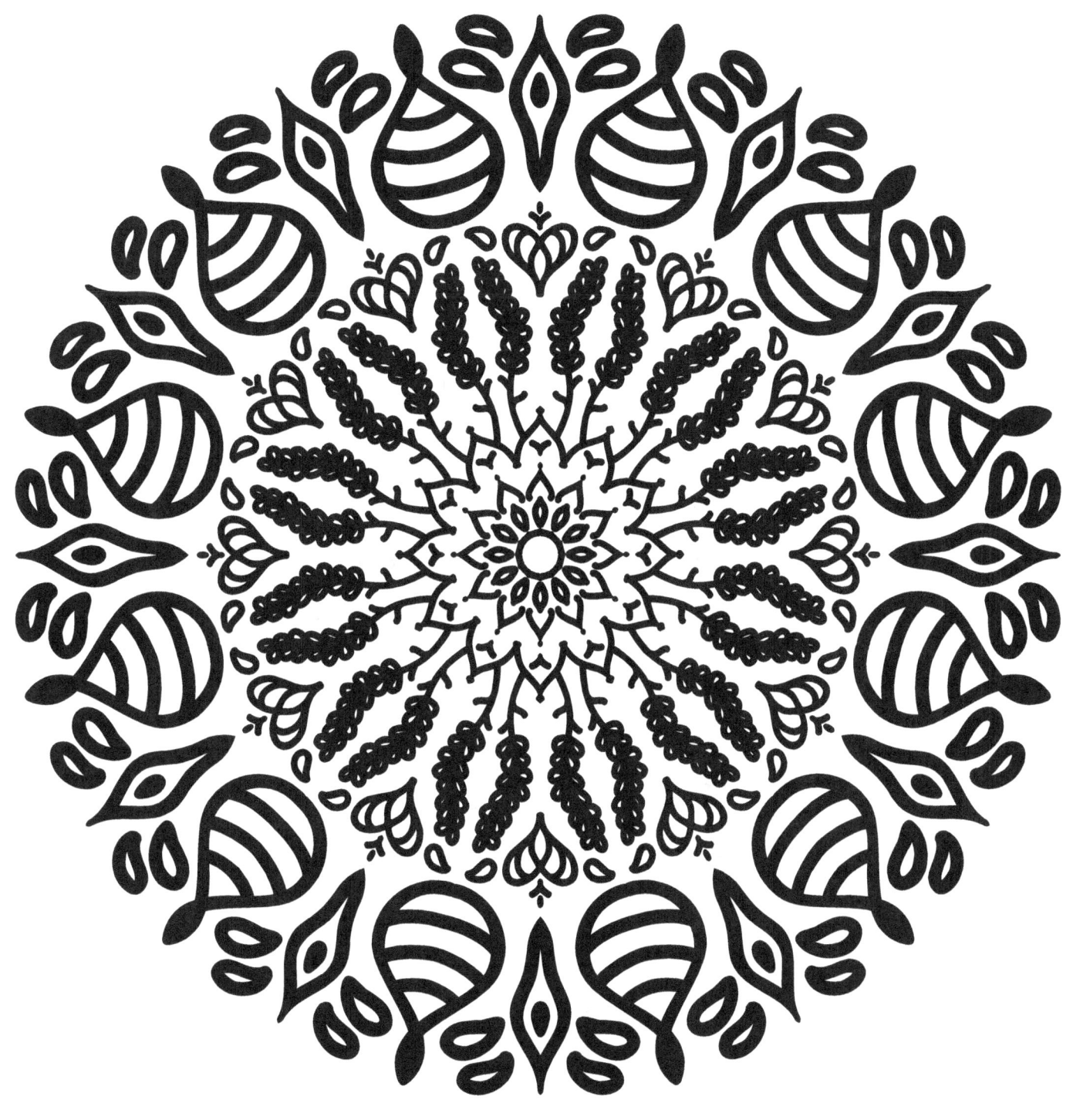

THINK
POSSITIVE

by Lili
Marlenn

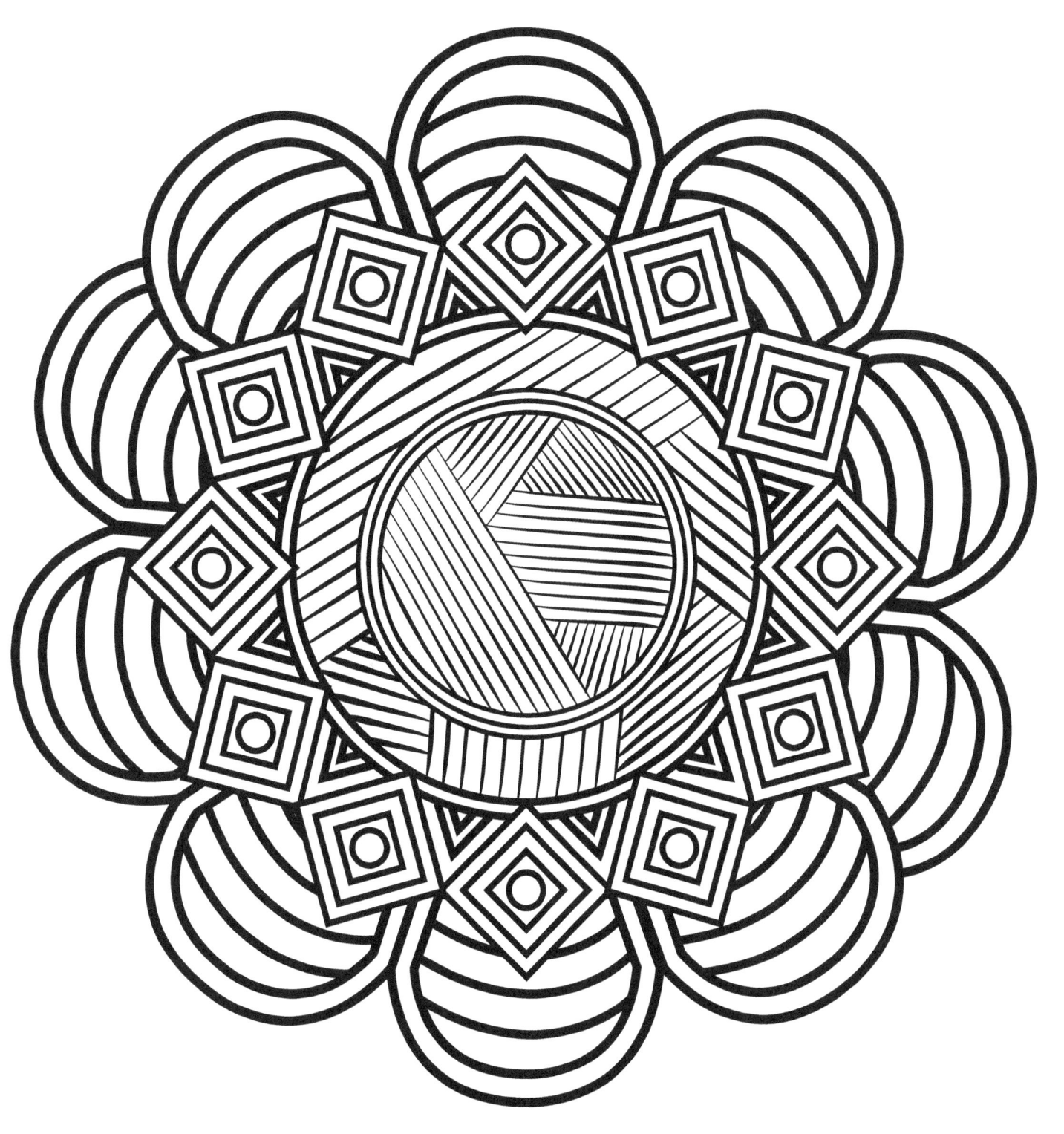

YOU LOOK GREAT

by Lili
Marlenn

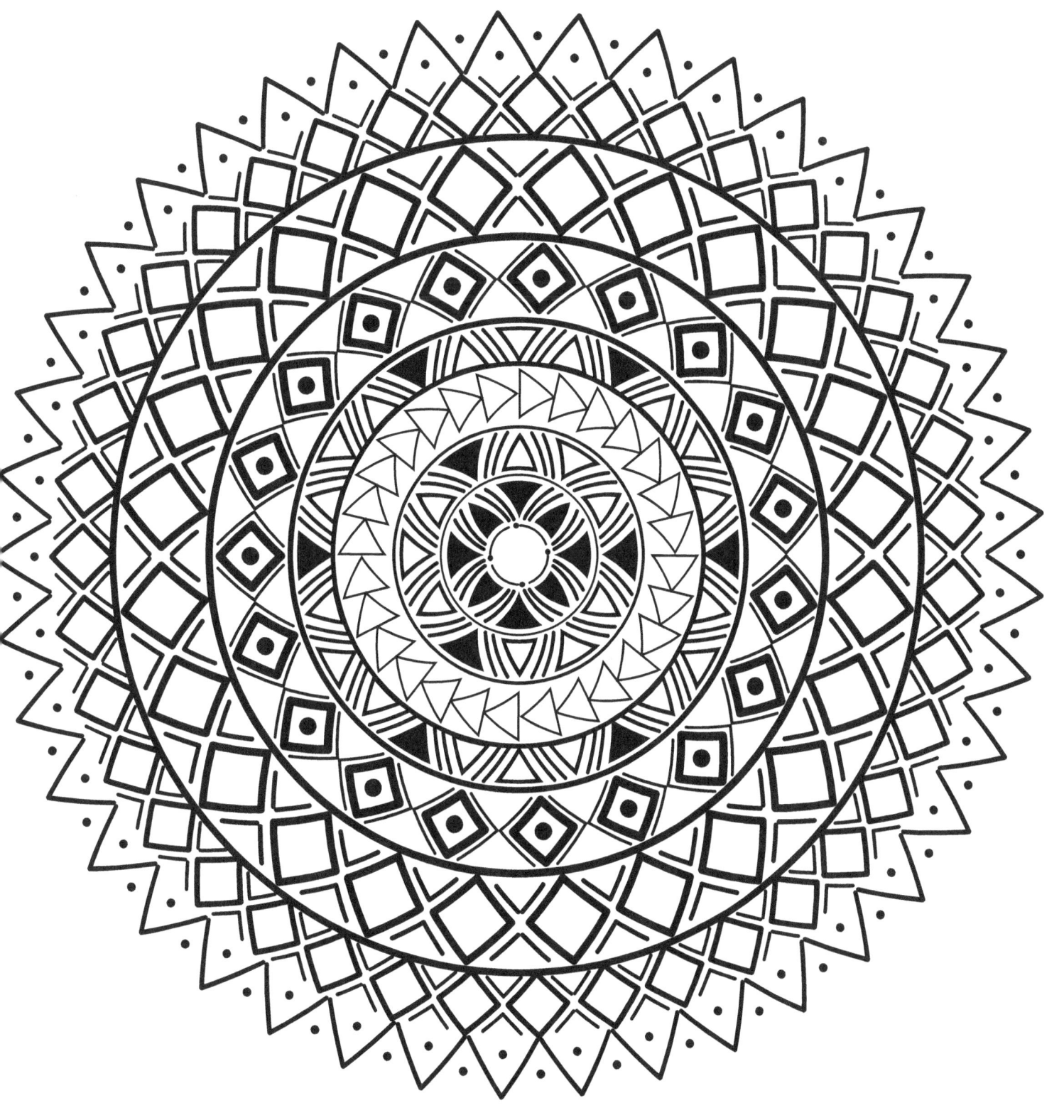

FOLLOW FOLLOW

by Lili
Marlenn

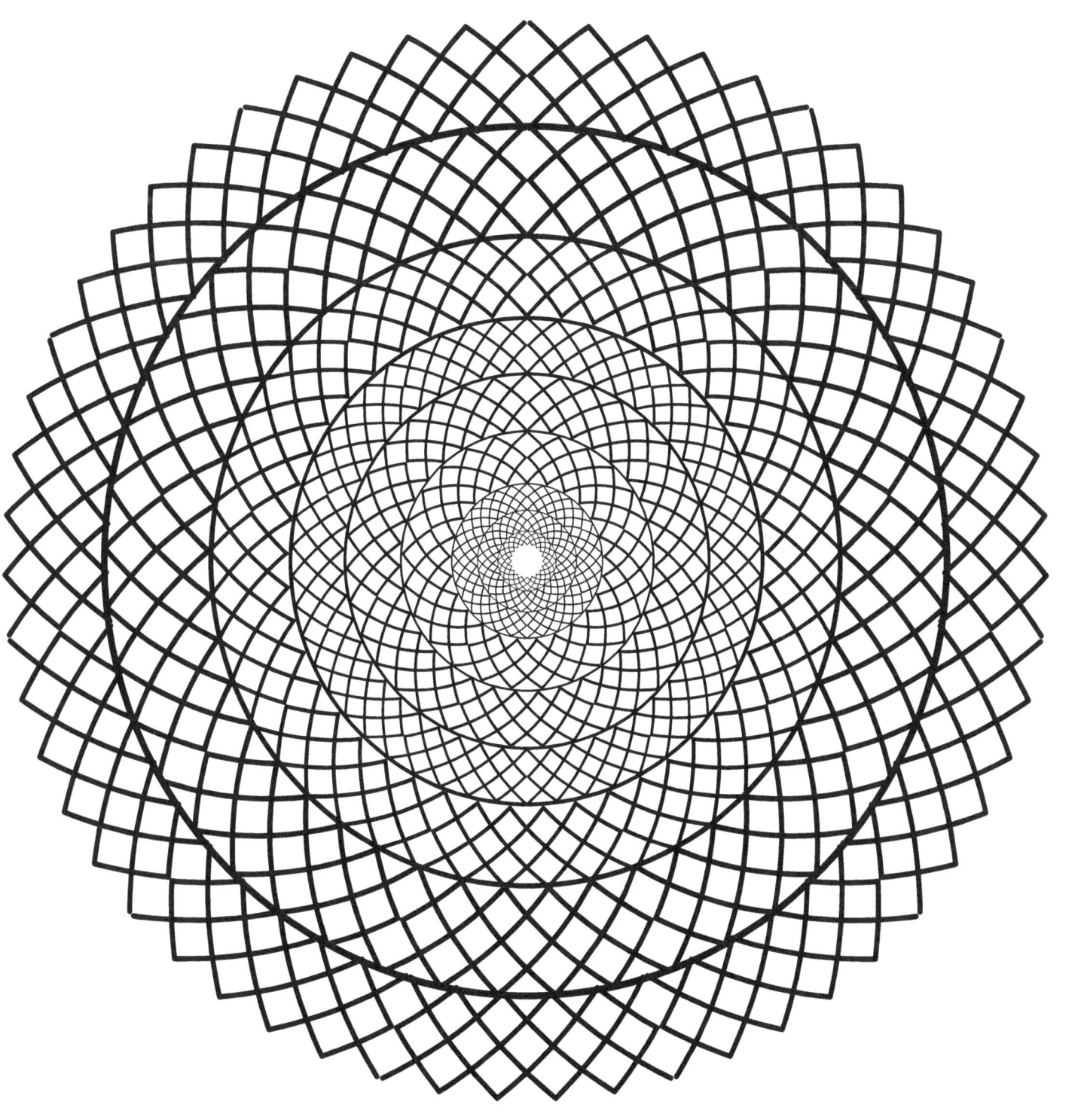

LOVE
PERFECTION
SATISFACTION

by Lili
Marlenn

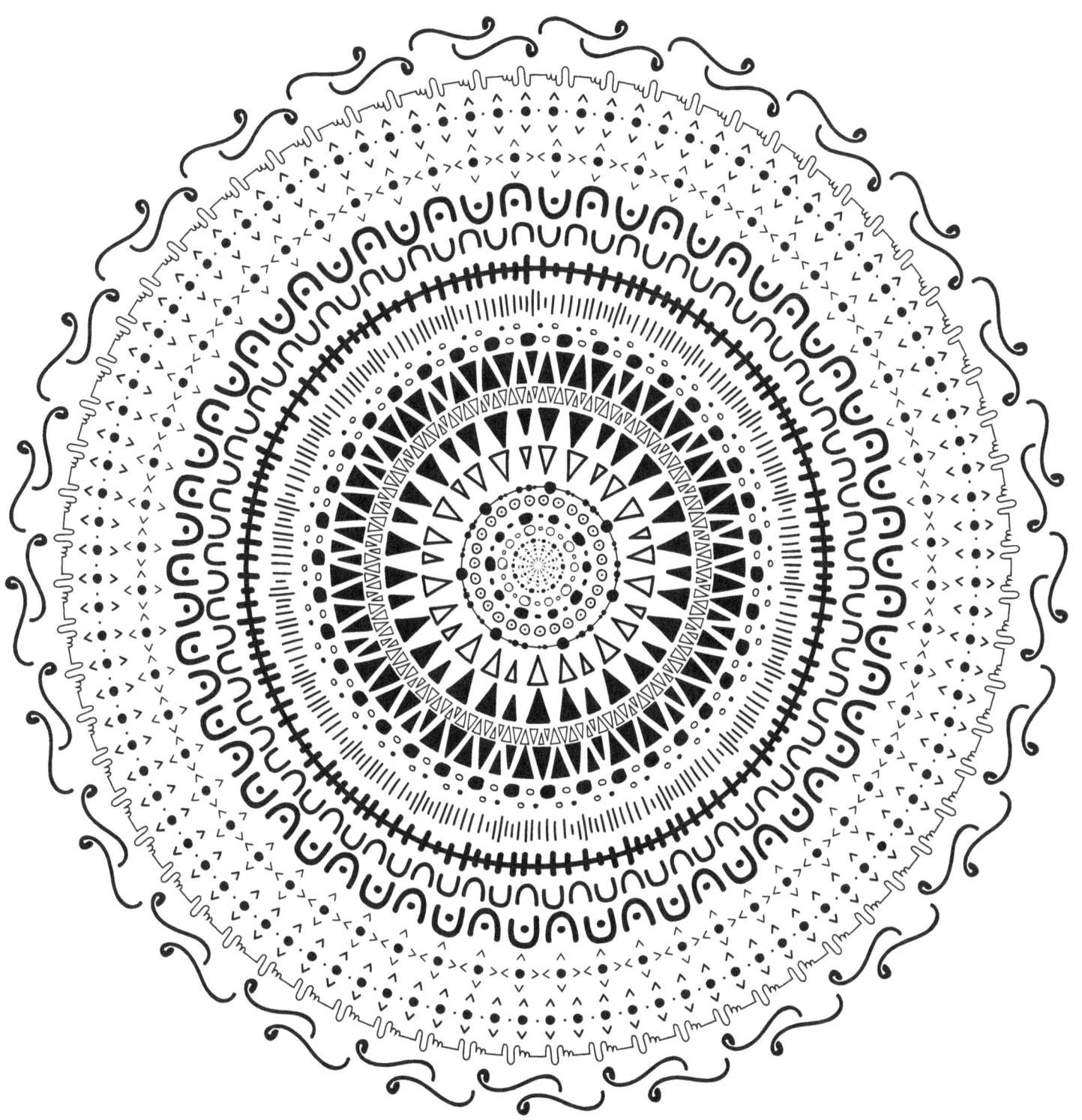

FAMILY

by Lili
Marlenn

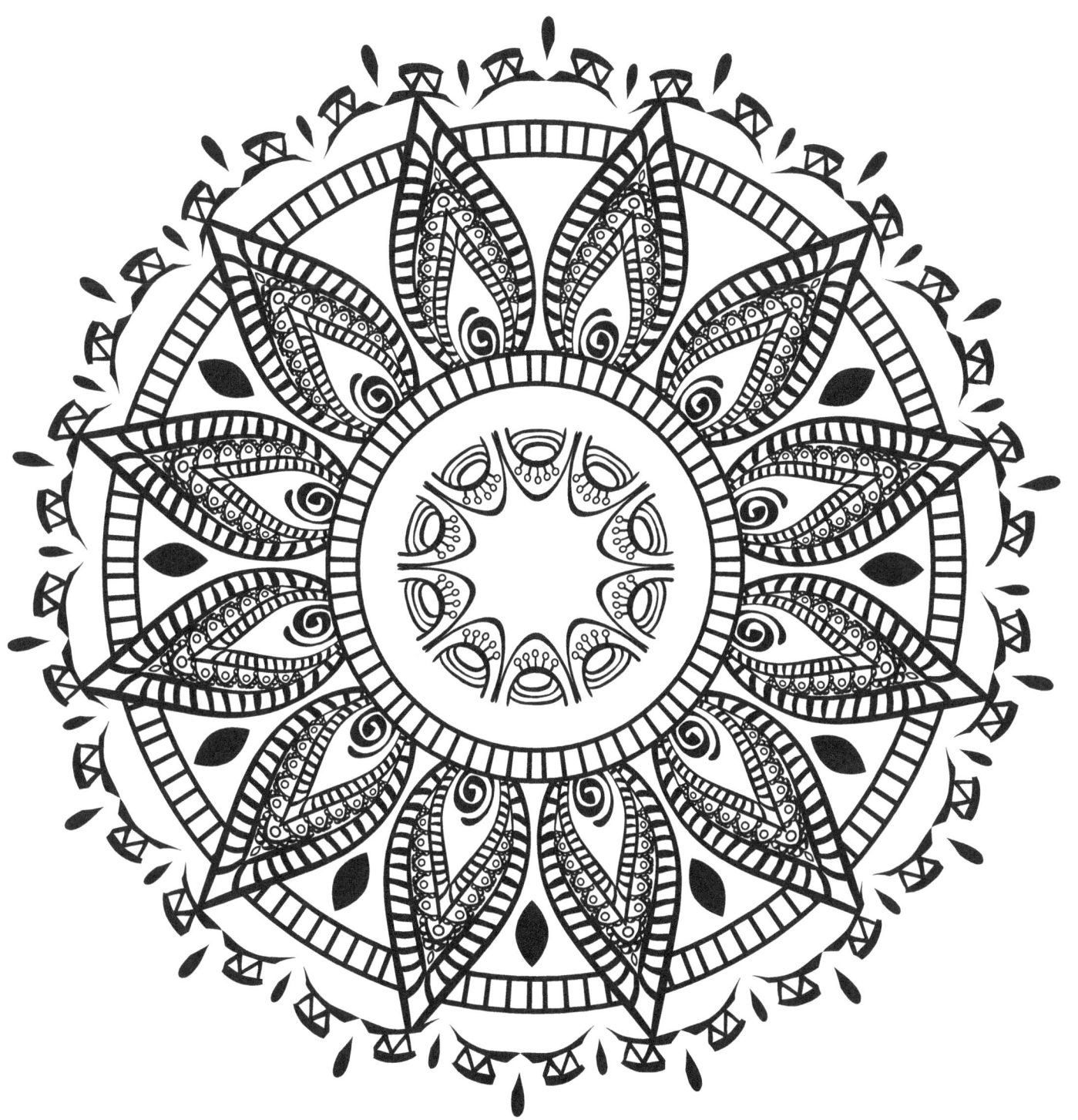

GOODNESS

by Lili
Marlenn

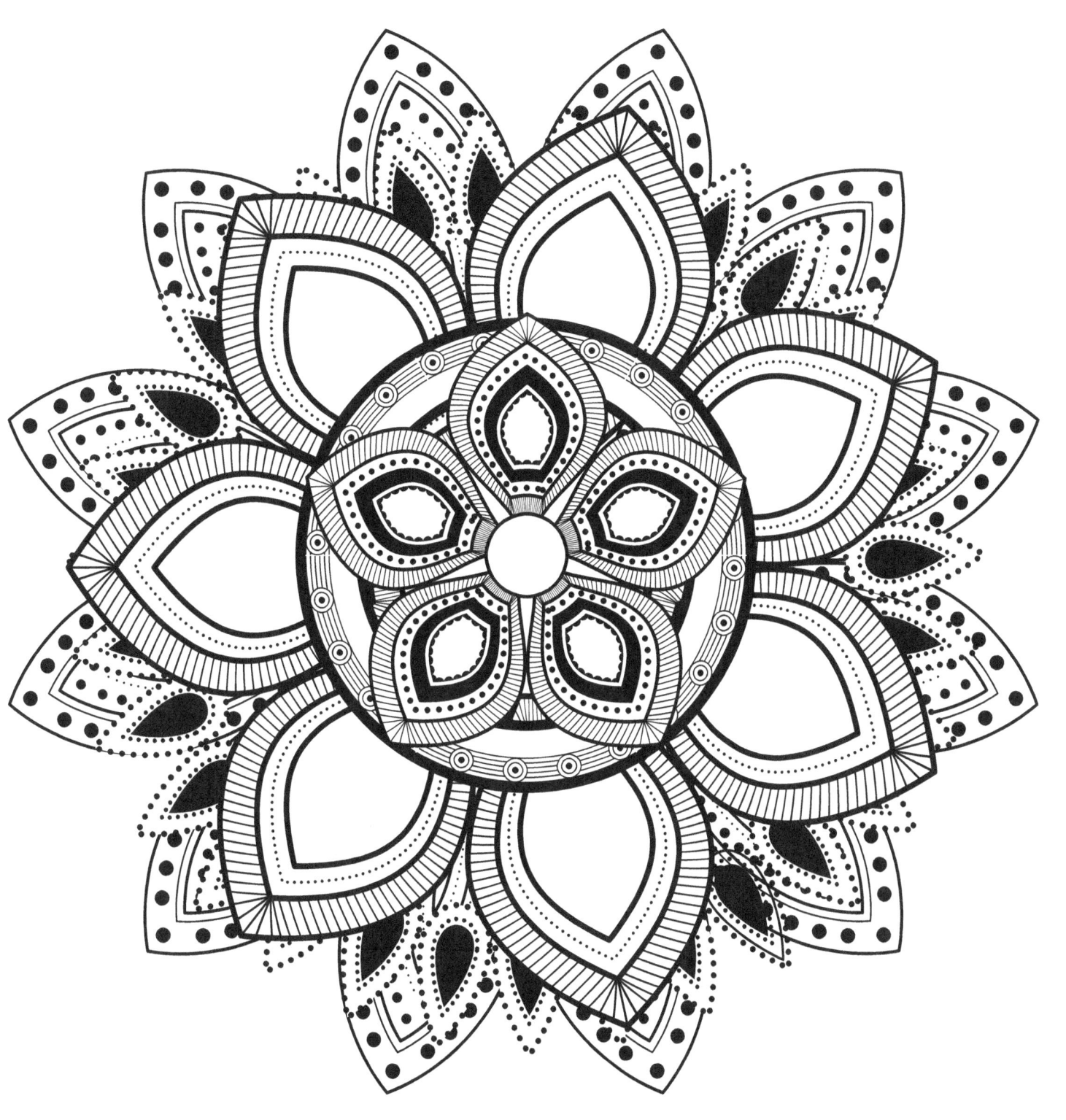

RELAX

by Lili Marlenn

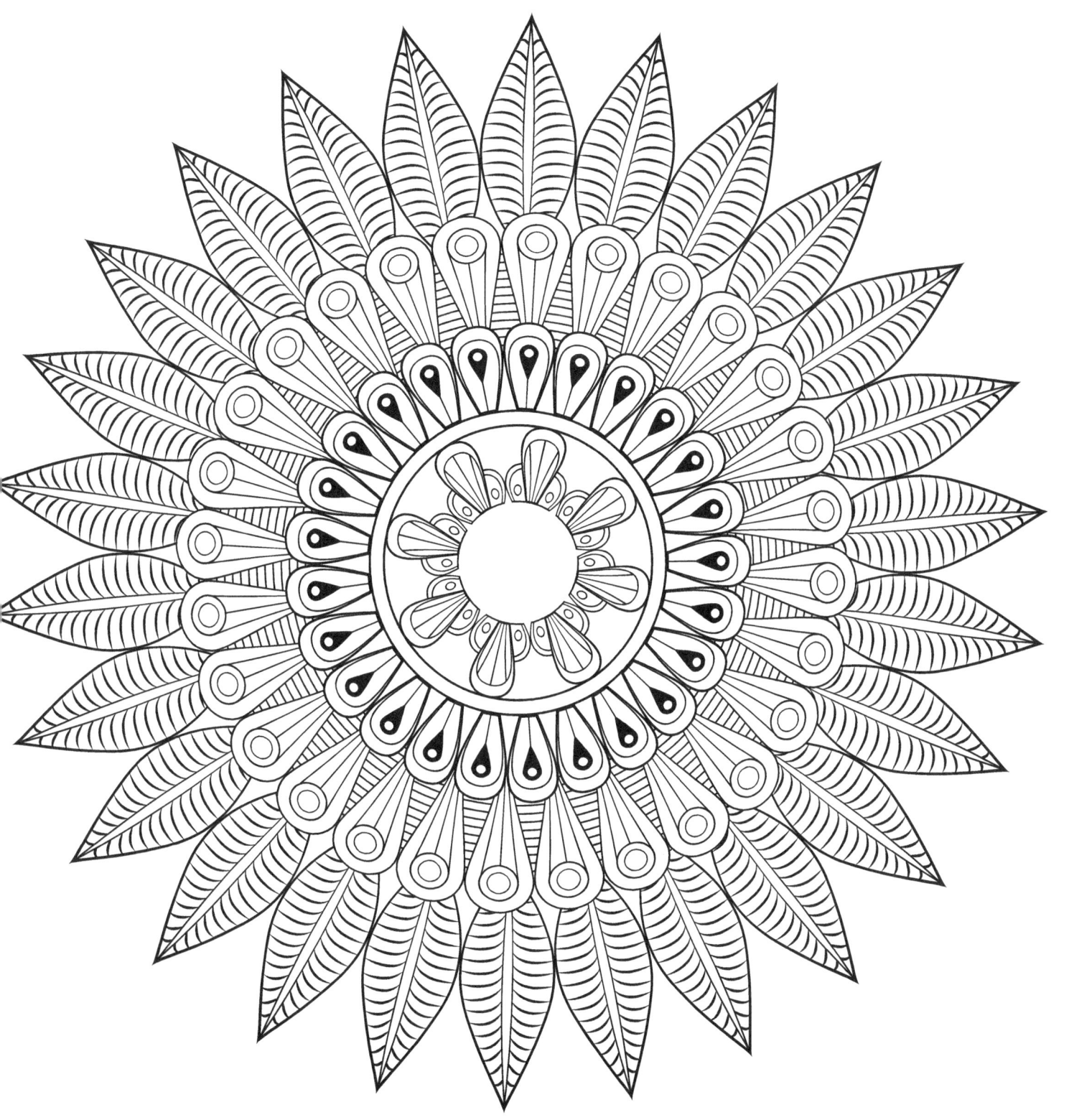

RELAX ONCE
AGAIN

by Lili
Marlenn

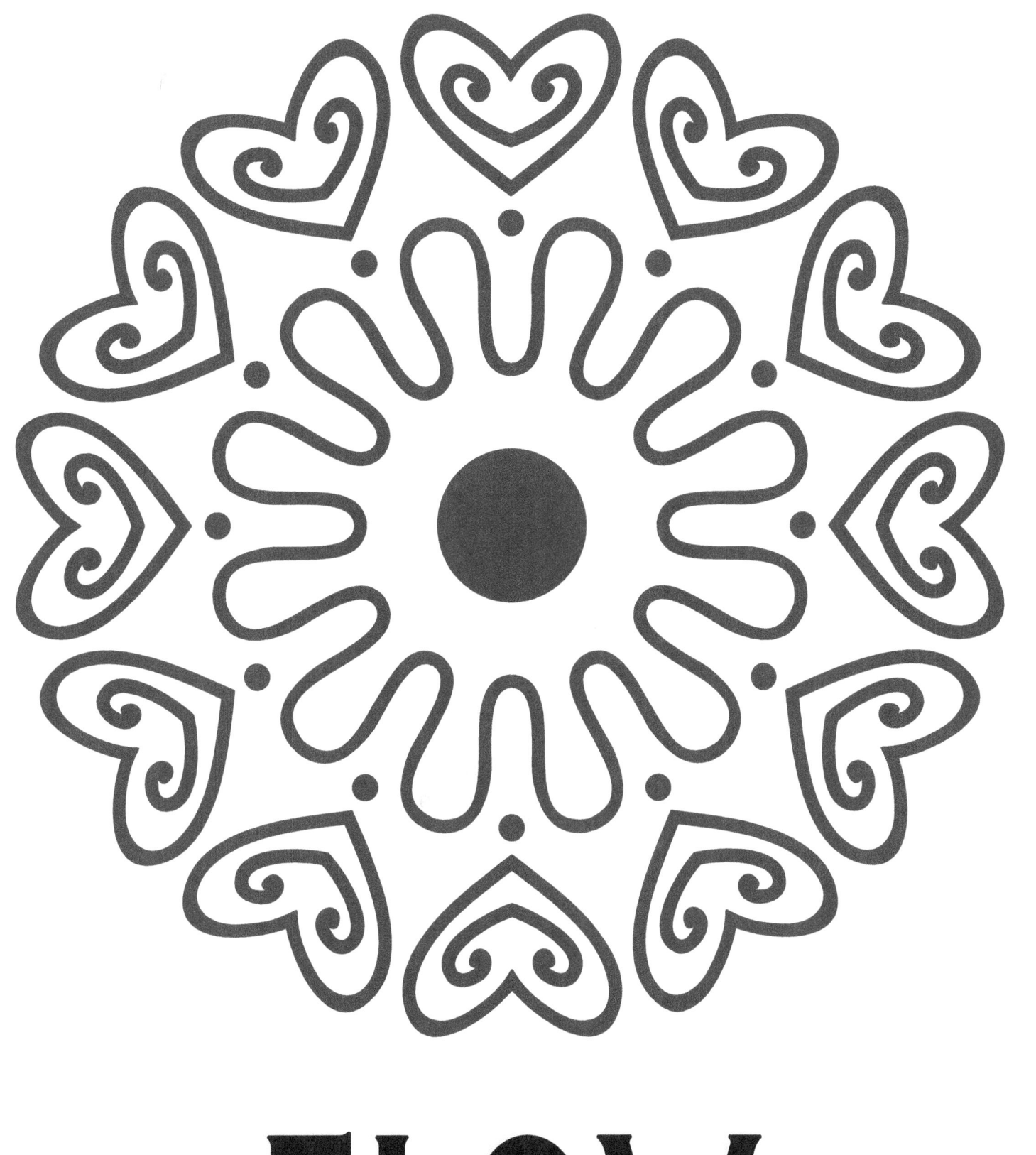

FLOW

by Lili
Marlenn

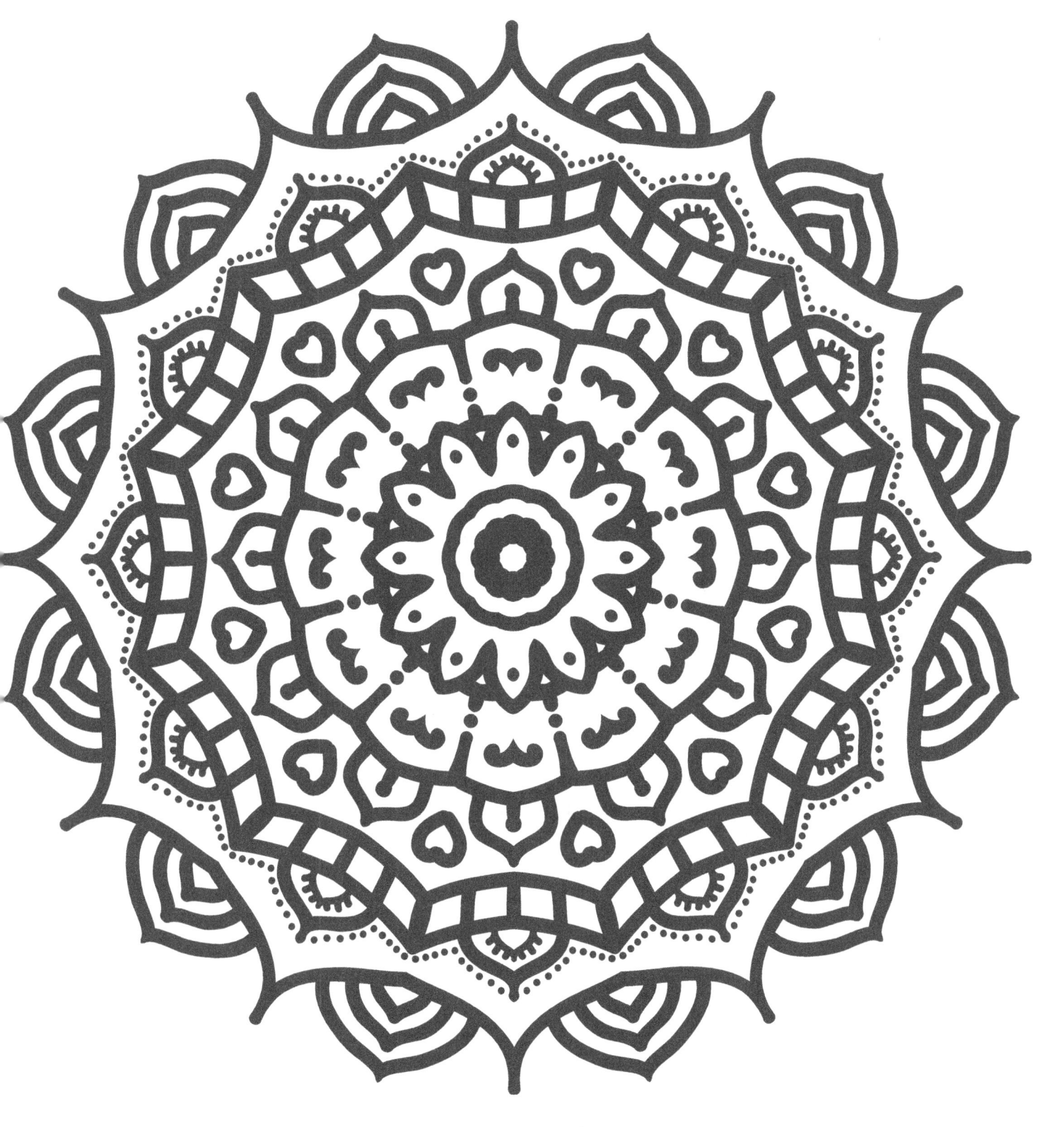

FUN

by Lili Marlenn

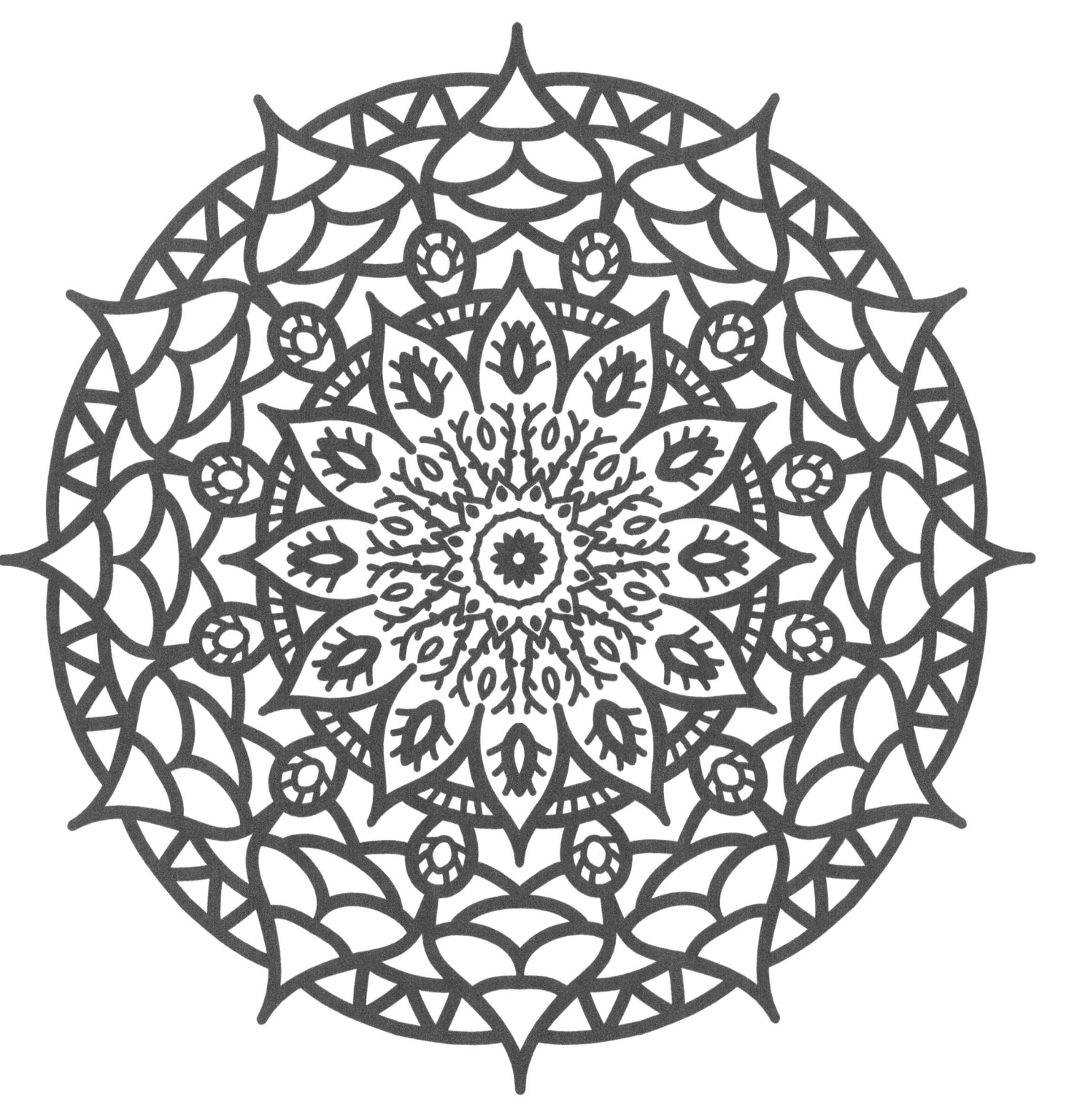

ENJOY

by Lili
Marlenn

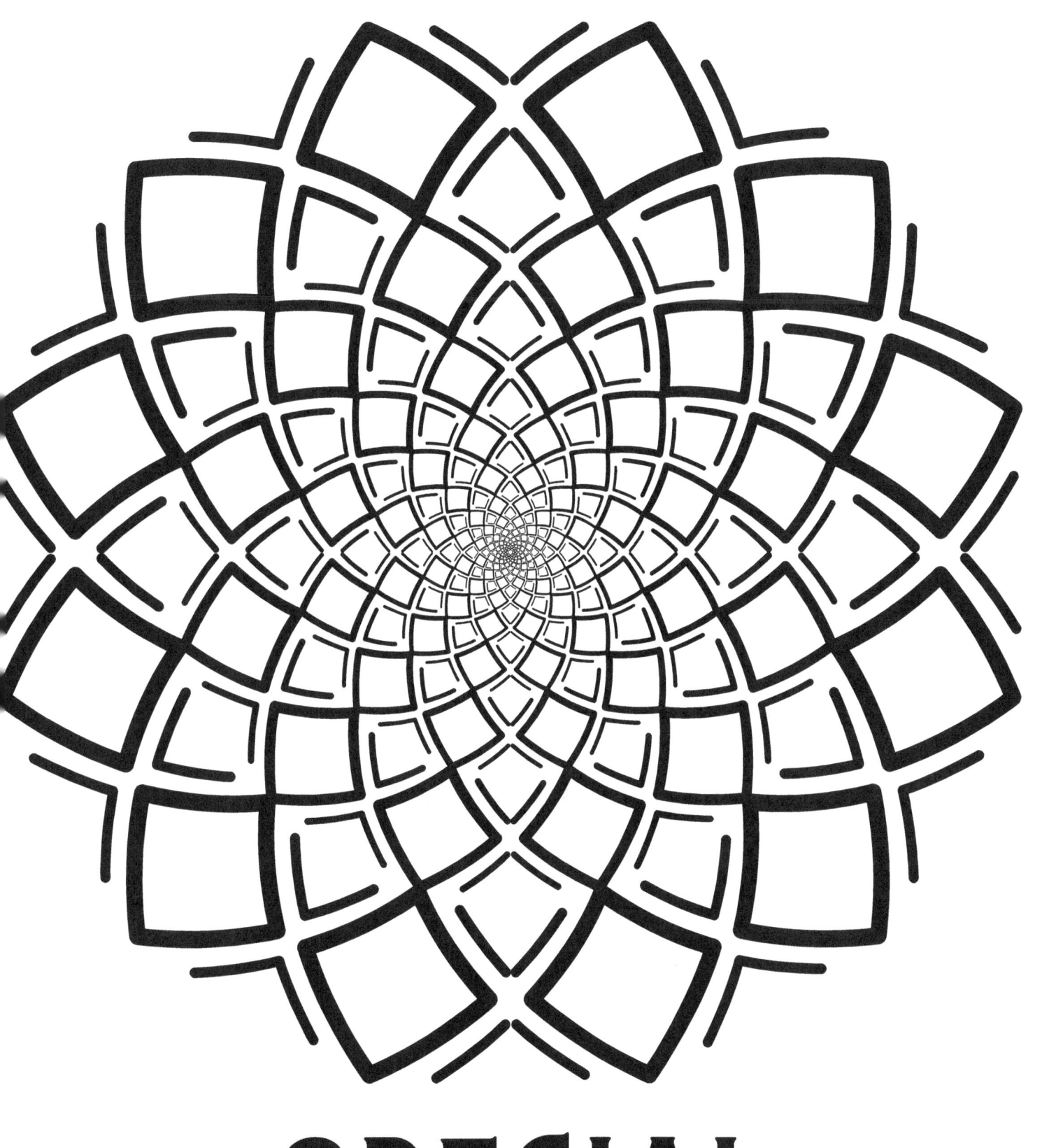

SPECIAL

by Lili
Marlenn

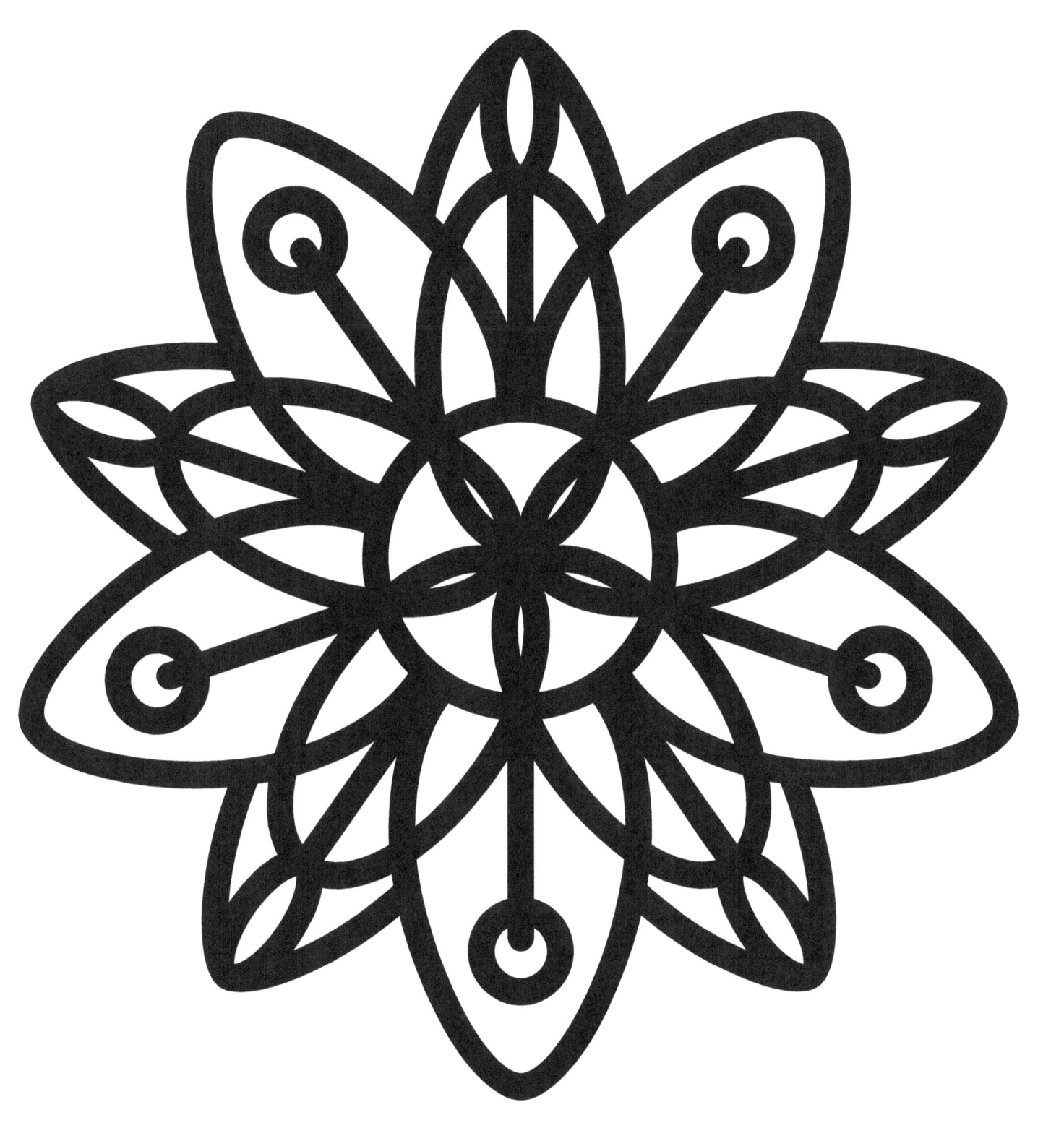

LET'S GO!

by Lili
Marlenn
thank you.